SUCCESSFUL PSYCHOTHERAPY

Successful
Psychotherapy

Edited by

JAMES L. CLAGHORN, M.D.

Assistant Director, Texas
Research Institute of Mental Sciences
Houston, Texas

PROCEEDINGS OF THE NINTH ANNUAL SYMPOSIUM, NOVEMBER 19-21, 1975
TEXAS RESEARCH INSTITUTE OF MENTAL SCIENCES

BRUNNER/MAZEL, *Publishers* • New York

616.8914
Su 1
c.

Library of Congress Cataloging in Publication Data
Main entry under title:

Successful psychotherapy.
 Includes bibliographies and index.
  1. Psychotherapy—Congresses.   I. Claghorn, James, 1935-   II. Texas
Research Institute of Mental Sciences.
RC480.S8   616.8'914   76-40123
ISBN 0-87630-133-2

MANUFACTURED IN THE UNITED STATES OF AMERICA

Contributors

LESTER BAKER, M.D.
Director, Clinical Research Center, Children's Hospital of Philadelphia; Professor of Pediatrics, University of Pennsylvania, School of Medicine, Philadelphia, Pennsylvania

ALVIN G. BURSTEIN, Ph.D.
Professor and Chief, Division of Psychology, Department of Psychiatry, The University of Texas Health Science Center at San Antonio, Texas

JAMES L. CLAGHORN, M.D.
Assistant Director, Texas Research Institute of Mental Sciences; Assistant Professor of Psychiatry, Baylor College of Medicine; Associate Professor of Mental Science, The University of Texas Graduate School of Biomedical Sciences, Houston, Texas

VIRGINIA DAVIDSON, M.D.
Assistant Professor of Psychiatry, Baylor College of Medicine, Houston, Texas

EDWIN E. JOHNSTONE, M.D.
Head, Outpatient Division, Texas Research Institute of Mental Sciences; Clinical Assistant Professor of Psychiatry, Baylor College of Medicine and The University of Texas Medical School at Houston, Texas

v

HELEN S. KAPLAN, M.D., Ph.D.
Head, Sex Therapy and Education Program, Payne-Whitney Clinic, New York Hospital-Cornell Medical Center, New York, N.Y.

GERALD L. KLERMAN, M.D.
Professor of Psychiatry, Harvard University Medical School and Massachusetts General Hospital; Superintendent, Erich Lindemann Mental Health Center, Boston, Massachusetts

RONALD LIEBMAN, M.D.
Psychiatrist-in-Chief, Children's Hospital of Philadelphia; Acting Medical Director, Philadelphia Child Guidance Clinic; Assistant Professor of Psychiatry and Pediatrics, University of Pennsylvania, School of Medicine, Philadelphia, Pennsylvania

LESTER LUBORSKY, Ph.D.
Professor of Psychology in Psychiatry, University of Pennsylvania, School of Medicine; Research Scientist, Eastern Pennsylvania Psychiatric Institute, Philadelphia, Pennsylvania

PHILIP R. A. MAY, M.D.
Professor of Psychiatry, University of California at Los Angeles; Chief of Staff, Program Evaluation, Research and Education, Veterans Administration Hospital, Brentwood, California

SALVADOR MINUCHIN, M.D.
Director, Family Therapy Training Center, Philadelphia Child Guidance Clinic; Professor of Child Psychiatry and Pediatrics, University of Pennsylvania, School of Medicine, Philadelphia, Pennsylvania

THOMM K. ROBERTS, Ph.D.
Chief, Day Treatment Center, Texas Research Institute of Mental Sciences, Houston, Texas

BERNICE L. ROSMAN, Ph.D.
Director of Research, Philadelphia Child Guidance Clinic, Philadelphia, Pennsylvania

GEORGE M. SIMPSON, M.B., Ch.B.
Principal Research Scientist in Psychiatry, Rockland State Hospital, Orangeburg, New York

ROBERT N. SOLLOD, Ph.D.
Assistant Professor of Psychology, New York University, New York, N.Y.

HANS H. STRUPP, Ph.D.
Professor of Psychology, Vanderbilt University, Nashville, Tennessee

HENRY TOMES, Ph.D.
Associate Professor and Director, Community Mental Health Center, Meharry Medical College, Nashville, Tennessee

PAUL WATZLAWICK, Ph.D.
Research Associate, Mental Research Institute; Clinical Assistant Professor, Department of Psychiatry and Behavioral Sciences, Stanford University School of Medicine, Palo Alto, California

MYRNA M. WEISSMAN, Ph.D.
Associate Professor of Psychiatry (Epidemiology), Yale University School of Medicine; Director, Depression Research Unit, Connecticut Mental Health Center, New Haven, Connecticut

Contents

Introduction

From the time of Hammurabi there are documented evidences of "priest-doctors" who provided treatment consisting of medicinals, largely water, and incantations and religious exorcism. Through the powerful suggestive influence created by the social status of the practitioner, these had profound effects on the state of mind and psychosomatic functioning of patients. The tradition, which did not include a knowledge of anatomy and the dynamic aspects of nerve transmission and blood flow, relied instead on explanations based on humors flowing through the body.

The notion of humors appealed to the physicians of Greece as well, and Hippocrates evolved a psychological theory based on the humors he described of blood, phlegm, and black and yellow bile. Throughout antiquity, rest and respite from wordly cares provided relief for anxious, bored, depressed, and troubled human beings. As relaxing medicinals, including alcohol and the opiates, became available, they, combined with the personal attentions of healers and with respite from stress, became civilization's treatment for emotional distress.

It was not until the writings of Sigmund Freud that a theory truly related to the specific influences of the therapist evolved. Limited by knowledge of the time, the theory was further circumscribed by its controversial nature and the small number of people willing to commit themselves to its study. Psychoanalysis came to flower in the United States, augmented by the concept of a thera-pist's beneficial influence over another person's behavior. By iden-tifying specific conflicts and making unconscious material available to conscious recognition, by word association and dream analysis, the nonspecific sense of dysphoria of patients became understand-able. The theoretical positions of the time are perhaps less significant than are the concept of individualized and precise appraisal of the causal events that produce dysphoria and the design of specific, describable strategies for correcting these defects.

A variety of competing world views led to a number of theories of personality and a continued development of psychoanalytic theory until the mid-1950s, when the momentum of psychological develop-ment shifted back to drugs as it had done several times in the past. Perhaps most interesting, we now have our contemporary version of humoral theories growing out of attempts to explain the modes of action of medicinal preparations. At the same time, as if to retrace its historic footsteps, the search for psychotherapeutic knowledge began to explore nonspecific therapeutic influences again. Rogers and Truax and others attributed personality changes produced in psychotherapeutic sessions principally to the empathy, warmth, and unconditional positive regard shown patients by psychotherapists. The work, however, proved impossible to replicate, and the neces-sary qualifications for a developing science were not met.

As Hans Strupp points out in the first chapter of this book, a science requires objective measurement, reproducibility of investiga-tions, and is above all a public enterprise. Although the experimental work of the 1950s was public, it failed to meet the criteria of replicability, invalidating the initial conclusions of investigators who believed they had identified the active ingredients of the psycho-therapeutic process. An unfortunate consequence of this faltering early scientific enterprise was a period of strong negative feeling about psychotherapy. Patently hostile studies discredited the age-old practice of one person's counseling another in times of distress. More recently, the introduction of behavior modification and the rigid structure imposed on investigators by the demands of psycho-pharmacological research brought studies that meet the requirements for objectivity of measurement and replication.

The present tone of the psychotherapeutic enterprise is ecumenical. Biofeedback, behavior modification, psychotropic drugs, and the specific and nonspecific aspects of psychotherapy are now seen in the public mind as component parts of a potential individual prescription. But they require a significant shift in the practitioner's attitude. The "priest-doctor" role is no longer an adequate model. Mystical powers are not discouraged or forbidden but are part and parcel of the nonspecific therapeutic repertoire. The therapist must specify as exactly as possible the areas of personal dysfunction for which a remedy is sought and develop a hierarchy of priorities for therapeutic intervention.

The recipe for intervention can now be viewed as multiple and as varied as the needs of the patient. Understanding the importance of systems large and small has led therapists to reevaluate the importance of the social system created by marriage and to understand and treat sexual dysfunctions. The significance of social and economic class and of stereotypes with regard to sex, race, and economic-role behavior has broadened the therapist's responsibility beyond the traditional. In the priestly tradition it was necessary for a learned professional to uncover the potential therapist's blind spots created by his own intrapsychic conflicts. Once these personal difficulties were unroofed and the healing process under way, a therapist could be certified as complete, whole, and ready for practice. Now it is the obligation of professionals, to themselves and to those they train, to be equally diligent in unroofing unrealistic, rigid and distorted views of men, women, blacks, the poor, the rich, the advantaged, the disadvantaged, the great and the humble. Combined with the growing body of techniques in which therapists must be trained, this emphasizes more than ever the need for continued individual professional growth and predicts that clinical psychiatry and psychology will experience the same degree of subspecialization that has occurred in other professional fields. The need to collect experimental data in reproducible fashion, to make that information public, and to accumulate knowledge in an orderly and critical fashion has never been as great.

To cover such diverse topics, we invited a panel of experts to present their philosophies, ideologies, research and treatment approaches at the ninth annual symposium of the Texas Research Institute of Mental Sciences. Of necessity, some growing fields of therapy are not covered, but we trust the reader will feel that the areas included are well selected.

Psychotherapy for schizophrenia had a high priority. Philip May stresses the importance of integrating chemotherapy with psychotherapy. George Simpson outlines the hazards of no treatment, insufficient treatment, or inappropriate treatment. Edwin Johnstone emphasizes the need for avoiding a custodial atmosphere in outpatient treatment by emphasizing goal-setting, and aggressive, reality-oriented psychotherapy combined with appropriate drug treatment. Gerald Klerman explores the varying theoretical positions as he clarifies the scientific principles of combining chemo- and psychotherapy. Lester Luborsky illustrates the scientific search for the active ingredient in therapy in his study of patient-therapist relationships.

Robert Sollod explains how sex therapy has come of age in the mid-1970s, having evolved from a ponderous, mechanistic approach to a synthesis of behavioral, psychodynamic, and interpersonal components through the work of Helen Singer Kaplan. Virginia Davidson explores the complex matter of patients' preferences for male or female therapists, finding that when a patient does declare a preference, the patient's age, sex, and marital status may be influencing factors. Compatibility of patient and therapist may weigh heavily on the outcome of therapy, and since attitudes about sexual roles are changing, these matters demand continual scrutiny, reflection, and study.

Analyzing a population of women seeking treatment, Myrna Weissman finds that since depressed women predominate in outpatient clinics, the study of traditional and unconventional approaches to depression is inextricably related to some conditions unique to the role of women. She suggests that while traditional approaches are efficacious for treating the clinical episode of depression, new approaches directed to the causative elements that make women depression-prone may prove to be more effective for prevention.

Alvin Burstein's use of the term "tonypandy" exposes two widely held myths about mental health services for poor people: the alleged inappropriateness of insight-oriented therapy for this group, and the claim that indigenous paraprofessionals can effectively substitute cultural congruence for formal training. Confronted by fact, we are forced to conclude that cultural differences pose problems that are amenable to some relatively simple educational efforts, and that, since there is no substitute for solid professional training, we must commit ourselves to professional mental health services for the poor.

Paul Watzlawick demonstrates that effectiveness in therapy may depend upon a change in the frame of reference (the meaning and value that a patient attributes to a particular reality). He illustrates specific behavioral prescriptions for "reframing" the ingredients of reality that distress the patient, and contends that our theories about "reality" determine what is possible to attempt or to achieve in therapy. Some "intractable" clinical problems may be effectively (even easily) treated if a fresh view of the problem lends itself to an unconventional intervention. Bernice Rosman, Salvador Minuchin, Ronald Liebman, and Lester Baker report dramatic improvement in patients suffering from anorexia nervosa when the therapy aims at restructuring the family system.

Henry Tomes explains how cultural attitudes and racism influence not only the content and style of treatment offered members of minority groups, but also influence some groups, black men in particular, to end treatment after only a brushing contact. He argues for a revolutionary change in the training of psychotherapists to deepen their understanding of and relationships to patients unlike themselves.

Successful psychotherapy, then, depends on a compatible matching of a particular patient with a suitably qualified, competent therapist. There is no substitute for rigorous professional training to master technical skills and theoretical expertise. The greater the therapist's ability to handle theoretical concepts, the greater her or his versatility in synthesizing a truly therapeutic approach with each patient's unique needs. Theoretical-technical training is only half the story, however. A therapist must be able to appreciate the patient's particular cultural role, and to respond in a fashion that is compatible with the patient's culturally determined attitudes, fears, needs, and frame of reference.

ACKNOWLEDGMENTS

We are grateful to the George and Mary Josephine Hamman Foundation, Lederle Laboratories, New England Nuclear Corporation, and Tenneco, Inc. for their generous financial support of the symposium. Special thanks to Joseph C. Schoolar, director of the Texas Research Institute, for his guidance of the symposium series, and to administrator Frank Womack and his staff for organizational support. Myrna Harlan accomplished the many secretarial duties; Lore Feldman, Meredith Riddell, and Linda Roberts copyedited the manuscript. To Louis A. Faillace, Charles M. Gaitz, Eugene Ebner, and Lou Ann Todd Mock many thanks for keeping the conference on course by chairing the sessions.

JAMES L. CLAGHORN
EDWIN E. JOHNSTONE

Part I

RELATIONSHIPS BETWEEN
PSYCHOTHERAPY AND
PHARMACOTHERAPY
IN SCHIZOPHRENIA

1

Themes in Psychotherapy Research

HANS H. STRUPP, Ph.D.

There are probably few areas of scientific interest in which confusion continues to flourish at such a high level as in psychotherapy (including such prominent subareas as psychoanalysis and behavior therapy). Despite decades of persistent debate, the advent of new techniques, theoretical writings, and, alas, voluminous empirical studies, the basic issue relating to the nature of the therapeutic influence and its effects remains as foggy as ever.

The fundamental problem which has proven so utterly refractory is that we are trying to assess the effects of exceedingly complex human interactions that are structured such that one person (therapist) attempts to influence or modify the feelings, cognitions, and behavior of another (patient). We then set ourselves the task of ascertaining whether the therapist's interventions have produced a measurable effect on the patient, with the proviso that the changes must be relatively permanent. Temporary or transient changes are considered trivial and ruled out as legitimate goals. This paradigm guides the operations of orthodox psychoanalysis, as well as those of the most confirmed behavior therapist; to some extent, although with qualifications, it is equally applicable to the "human potential" movement and to "growth" experiences of various kinds. Thus, we exclude from consideration those interpersonal activities (e.g., religious and educational experiences) , in which the therapeutic effects of the psychological mechanisms are not a primary concern, and we

3

arrive at the basic scientific problem: *What kinds of changes occur as the result of the interventions we lump under the heading of psychotherapy, and what is the nature of the psychological forces to which such changes may be attributed?*

By stating the problem in this manner, we are also asserting that psychotherapy is a set of phenomena which may be fruitfully studied by the scientific method on which Western society has come to rely as the most trustworthy ally in advancing human knowledge and dispelling ignorance, preconception, superstition, and myth. Psychotherapy is a science to the extent that it subscribes to the propositions that answers to basic questions come from the disciplined study of empirical data, and that principles must derive from unbiased observation and, if possible, from controlled experimentation. The study of psychotherapy is in principle no different from scientific efforts to understand problems of photosynthesis, echolocation in bats, or the effectiveness of a pharmacological substance. The fact that the principles of psychotherapy are of immediate and continuing interest to the practicing therapist merely underlines the urgency of research and its great social importance; it has nothing to do with the problem of how valid knowledge is obtained or with the perennial schism between researchers and practitioners.

To be sure, the practicing clinician as an applied scientist cannot wait until the researcher supplies him with all the answers he might need—this may never be possible. The exigencies of clinical practice are always such that he must do the best he can with the limited knowledge at his disposal. At the same time, however, he must be capable of tolerating considerable uncertainty, and he must see his techniques and his interventions and their theoretical underpinnings as tentative, provisional, and subject to modification in the light of emerging knowledge.*

I may be accused of stating the obvious and rehearsing elementary

---

* Compare Bronowski's (1973) formulation of this problem with respect to the physical sciences: "One aim of the physical sciences has been to give an exact picture of the material world. One achievement of physics in the twentieth century has been to prove that that aim is unattainable. . . . There is no absolute knowledge. And those who claim it, whether they are scientists or dogmatists, open the door to tragedy. All information is imperfect: We have to treat it with humility. That is the human condition, and that is what quantum physics says. . . ."

principles of scientific investigation. What seems to justify my observations are the following considerations: 1) Research in psychotherapy has frequently been viewed by clinicians as an esoteric pursuit that has little perceptible bearing on the complex phenomena with which the therapist, of necessity, has to deal, a luxury the clinician can opt to accept or disregard; 2) since the time of Freud's revolutionary insights the method of clinical observation has been regarded as the prime and optimal source of knowledge for clinical and therapeutic phenomena; and 3) with the proliferation of theories and techniques, sight has frequently been lost of the necessity to subject the phenomena to rigorous study and scrutiny. Another way of stating the problem is to assert that the role and function of scientific investigation have been poorly understood by many practitioners, that the demonstrated value of existing knowledge has tended to be greatly overestimated, and that, because of the difficulties, tedium, and slow progress of scientific investigation, uncertainty and skepticism which should be the stock in trade of applied professionals have often been replaced by conviction in the validity of criteria that are based on shaky and questionable evidence.

In a characteristic passage, presently to be quoted, Freud (1933) stated, without developing fully, his views about the preferred method of investigation in psychotherapy and psychoanalysis, the role of "research" as he understood it, and the nature of scientific evidence. In other writings, toward the end of his career, Freud rested content with the assertion that the nature of therapeutic action in psychoanalysis had been well understood, and that there was little else to be learned from study of that subject. I will take up that theme a bit later, but first let me quote the passage I mentioned:

> I have never been a therapeutic enthusiast. . . . Psychoanalysis is really a method treatment like others. It has its triumphs and defeats, its difficulties, its limitations, its indications. At one time a complaint was made against analysis that it was not to be taken seriously as a treatment since it did not dare to issue any statistics of its successes. Since then, the Psycho-Analytic Institute in Berlin, which was founded by Dr. Max Eitingon, has published a statement of its results during its first ten years. Its therapeutic successes give

grounds neither for boasting nor for being ashamed. But statistics of that kind are in general uninstructive; the material worked upon is so heterogeneous that only very large numbers would show anything. It is wiser to examine one's individual experiences. And here I should like to add that I do not think our cures can compete with those of Lourdes. There are so many more people who believe in the miracles of the Blessed Virgin than in the existence of the unconscious. . . . Analysis as a psychotherapeutic procedure does not stand in opposition to other methods used in this specialized branch of medicine; it does not diminish their value or exclude them. . . . It is in fact technique that necessitates the specialization in medical practice . . . (pp. 151-152).

A few observations appear to be in order:

1. While Freud recognized that the public had a right to be informed concerning the "statistics of [psychoanalysis's] successes" and applauded the Berlin Institute's primitive efforts at compiling data on treatment outcomes (therapists' overall judgments of patients grouped in various diagnostic categories) , characterizing the findings as moderately encouraging, he promptly rejected such forays as "in general uninstructive." He was not troubled by the problems to which the contemporary researcher in psychotherapy is giving serious attention, such as: What constitutes "improvement" or lack of improvement in psychotherapy? What are the determinants of therapists' judgments of "improved" or "unimproved"? Can the therapist, who is ego-involved, be accepted as the sole or the ultimate source of criterion information? What sources of bias influence his assessments? Can retrospective ratings be accepted as reliable evidence? What steps must be taken to guard against faulty inference?

2. The reasons Freud gave for rejecting "statistics" are a) the heterogeneity of the patient material, and b) the problem of small samples. The contemporary researcher of course appreciates the fact that, in addition to these problems, there are many other sources of error, but it is characteristic that Freud opted not for better research but instead reaffirmed *clinical experience* as the ultimate recourse for evaluating the effectiveness of one's professional work,

and, by implication, for advancing the scientific understanding of clinical phenomena.

Freud's low opinion of "statistics" is certainly understandable in the light of the rudimentary state of knowledge of behavioral science and clinical research at the time. To be sure, more than any clinician before him or since, he had just cause to take pride in the enormous fruitfulness of the clinical method in the hands of a sensitive, acute, and insightful clinical observer. Freud, however, failed to appreciate the *limitations* inherent in his preferred approach. The clinical method assuredly had served him well, and it had been the source of inspirations, insights, and hypotheses of unprecedented penetration and promise. As far as he was concerned, there remained no basic questions concerning the *modus operandi* of psychoanalysis, and on the basis of his clinical observations he felt justified—in the same passage quoted above—to draw comparisons between it and other methods of treatment. From such a comparison he emerged with the conclusion that psychoanalysis as a method of treatment was *primus inter pares,* that its results were at least as good as those achievable by other methods of treatment, and uniquely valuable under certain *specific* conditions. The latter he recurrently dealt with in his writings, the last time in "Analysis Terminable and Interminable" (Freud, 1937) (one might wish that some of his followers had been similarly cautious!) .

In this penetrating but essentially pessimistic paper Freud attempted to differentiate factors that potentiate and interfere with a favorable outcome in psychoanalysis and other forms of psychological treatment, factors around whose elucidation contemporary research in psychotherapy is squarely built. In basic terms, these relate to 1) *the patient,* including the nature of his current problems, their severity, and their antecedents in the patient's life; 2) the technical aspects of the *treatment,* that is, the nature of the interventions by which modifications of the patient's psychological state and his behavior are being attempted; 3) the personality of the *therapist,* which forms an integral part of the technical interventions and constitutes a crucially important part of the therapeutic influence that is brought to bear; and 4) the *situational circumstances,* such as pressures from the patient's family, cost of treatment, distance from therapist, etc.

Singly, and particularly in combination, these factors relate to what has been called the "match" between patient, therapist, and treatment (Luborsky and Strupp, 1962). If we had more precise knowledge about the significance of these variables in a particular case, we would of course be in a better position to prognosticate the outcome of treatment, select particular patients for particular therapists, and gear the therapeutic operations to patient and circumstances in an optimal manner. During the last two or three decades researchers have identified a number of variables that augur well or poorly for treatment outcomes, but in evaluating the viability of a particular patient-therapist dyad, we must continue to rely on clinical judgment, which is the best we have, but which, we must hasten to add, is imprecise, fallible, and subject to a variety of errors.

THE CRITERION PROBLEM

The single most serious difficulty impeding research and clinical progress is the absence of consensus relating to criteria of outcome, and hence the measurement of change. As long as we have no firm anchors—reliable and valid measurements of the patient's functioning at the beginning and at some more or less arbitrary end point of treatment—we cannot make definitive statements concerning the changes a particular treatment or set of interventions has wrought, judge to what extent and in what areas a patient has changed, compare patients having been subjected to a particular treatment modality, and, perhaps most important, make comparisons between patients exposed to different forms of therapy, which would enable us to arrive at meaningful conclusions concerning their relative merit. In short, unless we can resolve the criterion problem, our therapeutic endeavors will remain indeterminate and the entire therapeutic enterprise will remain built on quicksand (Bergin, 1971).

As practicing clinicians we will undoubtedly have impressions, and our clinical experience can enlighten us up to a point, but until such time as we can establish the ground rules by which therapeutic successes and failures are to be judged, there will be disputes, polemics, and idiosyncratic judgments. Despite advances in methodology, research design, and the sheer number of studies from which various, albeit tentative and qualified, conclusions can be drawn, we are still struggling with fundamental questions to which no one has been able to supply satisfactory answers. In an important sense we are dealing with a definitional problem, which cannot be answered by empirical research.

In the paper cited earlier, Freud (1933) defined outcome (i.e., "the end of an analysis") along two dimensions (p. 219) : "First, [that] the patient shall no longer be suffering from his symptoms and shall have overcome his anxieties and inhibitions, and secondly, [that] the analyst shall judge that so much repressed material has been made conscious, so much that was unintelligible has been explained, and so much internal resistance conquered that there is no need to fear a repetition of the pathological processes concerned." Freud added that the second definition is much more ambitious, in that "the effect upon the patient has been so profound that no further changes would take place in him if his analysis were continued."

Therapists of most theoretical persuasions would probably agree on the first criterion of symptom improvement. It is indeed difficult to envisage a form of psychotherapy that would fail to subscribe to the proposition that the most significant measure of success is the elimination or substantial amelioration of the difficulties that brought the patient to therapy in the first place. In modern usage, Freud's first criterion would be expanded to include 1) intrapsychic change (e.g., the "anxieties" of which Freud speaks), and 2) behavioral change (e.g., Freud's reference to "inhibitions," which however must also include other behavioral criteria) . But how can such assessments be combined into a judgment of "improvement"? What weight is to be given to various components? What is to be done if a patient improves in some areas of functioning but not in others? By what standards can a given change be judged an improvement? Are not cultural values inextricably involved?

SPECIFICITY

In a comprehensive review of the literature Strupp and Bergin (1969) came to the conclusion that "some patients benefit substantially from psychotherapy whereas many others are poor prognostic risks" (p. 29). It became clear to us that 1) psychotherapy is neither a unitary process nor is it applied to a unitary problem; 2) patients, therapists, and measurable changes in each instance are not interchangeable units; 3) contrary to critics of psychotherapy (e.g., Eysenck, 1952) who alleged that most patients recover "spontaneously" from neurotic disturbances (viewed as analogous to the common cold), the "spontaneous remission" rate varies considerably across patient types; and 4) the relative effectiveness of various types of psychotherapy has yet to be demonstrated. In an earlier paper, Kiesler (1966) had alerted the field to the "uniformity myth," exemplified by such terms as "average psychotherapy," "average outcome," "average therapeutic skill," etc. Thus it became clear that unless we succeeded in specifying the nature of the problem to which psychotherapy is applied, and the nature of the therapeutic influence that is being brought to bear (which includes considerations of techniques as well as the personality of the therapist applying them), and achieved consensus on what constitutes acceptable therapeutic change, the question, "Is psychotherapy effective?" retained a fallacious viability even though it had no more meaning than the question, "Is internal medicine effective?"

Therapists must accept part of the responsibility for the confusion which has been exploited by invidious critics over the years. The reason is that practitioners have rarely been sufficiently clear and explicit about the goals in treatment, the routes (techniques) by which these goals are to be reached, and how one might assess when, whether, and to what extent real changes have occurred in the patient. I have traced elsewhere (Strupp, 1973) how Freud's conservative stance—recall he restricted the utility of psychoanalytic therapy to the so-called transference neuroses, and even there fairly stringently defined the technique's radius of applicability—gradually became transformed into the "broadening scope" of analytic therapy, with what I judge to be disastrous results for patients, the professional community, and the public at large. We are now witnessing a return to a more modest position whose motto has become the emphasis on specificity I have sketched in the foregoing.

WHAT KINDS OF CHANGES ARE REALISTIC?

The widespread disenchantment with intensive psychoanalysis is well known and needs no exemplification in this context. However, I hasten to add that as a wholesale indictment of the field it is grossly undeserved. My own belief is that with certain patients and under certain specific circumstances it remains the very best that human ingenuity has been able to devise. The very fact that this assertion remains unappreciated by a large segment of the professional community, not to mention the public, underscores my point that the demand for specificity has largely gone unheeded. If it were otherwise, we would have no difficulty in assenting to the proposition that intensive psychoanalytic psychotherapy is an impressive therapeutic instrument, provided a set of highly specific conditions are met. Nor would we have to confront the nonsensical statement—advanced not only by malevolent critics, but also frequently embraced by researchers—that the most incisive and radical form of psychotherapy works best for patients who least need it, or that the outcome of psychotherapy in general (sic!) is best when the patient is substantially "healthy" at the time of entry. Only gross ignorance of the frequently subtle but enormously pervasive destructiveness of neurotic conflicts, particularly in individuals who to all appearances appear to be "well functioning," can lead to such pat conclusions.

By contrast, it is a very different matter to assert that in order to be considered a suitable candidate for psychoanalytic therapy the patient must have considerable ego strength and meet other stringent conditions. Let us suppose that he does. For many years analysts have selected analysands with due regard to the complex problems traditionally subsumed under the heading "analyzability." Were it the case that these selection criteria, singly or in combination, had high predictive value for outcome, there would by now be little doubt in anyone's mind that analytic therapy produces radical and discernible personality and behavior change. In short, a substantial proportion of those entering intensive therapy would be impressive successes. As therapists we know that such cases exist, but they are not as numerous as we would like, and, for another matter, we have failed to impress the scientific and general community that the results justify the prodigious investment of time, effort, and money.

Several points should be added:

1. It is abundantly clear that the field as a whole has failed to adduce the kind of conclusive and ironclad evidence that can reasonably be demanded by the scientific community. While good studies are becoming somewhat more numerous, they are still the exception.

2. It may be asserted that many of the changes produced by intensive dynamic psychotherapy (including psychoanalysis) are so subtle that they cannot be adequately captured by clinical ratings and other psychometric instruments that are notoriously crude and overly inclusive. There is a certain cogency in this statement; however, granting that our instruments are not nearly as sensitive and precise as we would like them to be, if personality and behavior changes resulting from intensive therapy were really impressive, they would be captured even by crude assessment procedures. All that can be said is that in certain instances—no one really knows what percentage—significant therapeutic modifications have resulted, and there exists little doubt in the minds of patients or therapists that these changes are indeed attributable to the therapeutic operations under discussion. In other words, the changes are real; they are not due to so-called placebo effects, "nonspecific relationship factors," or changing conditions in the patient's life.

3. The stringent selection criteria alluded to in the foregoing are frequently not met, but the patient is accepted for treatment anyway. The rationale is that "perfect" patients are as much an ideal as "perfect" therapists or a "perfect" therapeutic instrument, and that even if the prognosis is not as favorable as it might be there are many reasons why such patients should nevertheless be accepted for therapy. In medicine the reputation of a physician is not based solely on his cure rate—in fact, patients often receive only palliative treatment, and indeed many patients die without the doctor being blamed for events over which he has no control. In other words, even if the outlook is at best modest the patient still has a right to be treated, but it then becomes a questionable issue whether relative failure should be charged against the method of treatment, as is typically done in psychotherapy outcome studies. Somehow, psycho-

therapists and psychotherapy are judged by their cure rate and the entire field is faulted if the track record is less than perfect. The question clearly has many other ramifications that cannot be pursued here.

4. Finally, there is the troublesome possibility that there is nothing wrong with the psychoanalytic treatment modality (or any other psychotherapeutic treatment modality) but there are relatively few therapists who are sufficiently well trained and whose personality characteristics are sufficiently congruent with the therapy. It is a disquieting thought that relatively few psychoanalysts may know how to conduct proper analyses, but I believe there is more than casual evidence to suggest that this statement is probably true. I shall presently return to this aspect of the problem.

As suggested earlier, the field has severely suffered from the persistent confusion surrounding criteria of outcome. Things were simple in Freud's day when therapists rested content to judge a patient "cured" or "greatly improved." Rightfully, questions have been raised concerning the ingredients of such judgments, the empirical indicators of improvement, the reliability and validity of assessments made by clinicians who have a vested interest, the precise nature of the changes on which a judgment of "improvement" is based, and, perhaps most important, whether the changes are indeed attributable to the operations to which therapists would like to credit them.

Consider but one of the difficulties: Despite protracted efforts to define and dimensionalize change measures, we are as yet unable to make reliable qualitative distinctions between changes resulting from ten sessions of "supportive" psychotherapy administered by a first-year resident or graduate student in a typical outpatient clinic or counseling center and 250 hours of intensive dynamically oriented psychotherapy, or for that matter orthodox analysis, conducted by a psychoanalyst with 25 years of experience. Clinical experience informs us that there must be differences between a person whose morale has been boosted by a therapist's respect, understanding, and empathy so that for the time being (or a longer period) he feels less anxious, depressed, and self-deprecating, as opposed to an individual who has undergone significant structural changes which have radically altered his self-concept and life-style, along with the symptoms that brought him to the attention of a therapist. The experienced clinician may feel that he is capable of making these distinctions, but we lack evidence to verify them. In light of these difficulties, it is not hard to understand that arguments persist about the kinds of changes that psychotherapy can produce, and we are frustrated in countering conceptualizations that equate the nature of the therapeutic influence with a benign human experience for which perhaps no rigorous technical training is required.

The sometimes not peaceful coexistence of theoretical viewpoints based on divergent assumptions lends credence to the assertions of those who subscribe to a reductionistic "nothing-but" position. The thoughtful therapist *thinks* he knows better, but how can he convince the skeptic?* The research literature supports the clinician's belief that therapeutic changes do occur under the "right" circumstances (i.e., a suitable patient, a reasonably competent and constructive therapist, and situational factors that are reasonably propitious), but this is a far cry from making the qualitative distinctions mentioned above. While at present and in the foreseeable future we are nowhere near that goal, I continue to subscribe to the hope that eventually it will be possible to develop instruments and assessment procedures of appropriate sensitivity, reliability, and validity. When this feat is accomplished I hope it will be possible to demonstrate that the changes occurring in a patient who has undergone intensive long-term therapy are in fact qualitatively different from the changes resulting from the typical short-term exposure in the average out-patient clinic. Both patients, no doubt, will be shown to "feel better" by crude measures, but there will be discernible and significant *structural* changes that are more radical, more incisive, and more lasting. Unfortunately, we are as yet not well equipped to assess such structures as the executive apparatus of the ego and the manner in which it mediates between cognitions, emotions, needs, wishes, and overt behavior.

---

* I am reminded of a comment by Gordon Allport: "The greatest failing of the psychologist at the present time is his inability to prove what he knows to be true."

TOWARD A CLARIFICATION OF SHORT-TERM GOALS

The question of quantitative and, more importantly, qualitative differences, over and beyond its theoretical interest, has important practical implications, to which I shall next turn.

Since the bulk of psychotherapeutic effort is invested in short-term treatment, and since there is an ever-growing interest in devising and sharpening treatment methods aimed at short-term interventions, it behooves us to achieve much greater clarity concerning the *nature* of such changes, what techniques are optimal to bring them about, and the limits which are set by factors in the patient, the treatment, the therapist, and the circumstances in which the therapy proceeds. Thus the specificity issue discussed earlier has tremendous practical significance.

In a long-term study currently in progress at Vanderbilt University, male college students are being treated for anxiety, depression, and shyness by relatively short-term psychotherapy (25 hours or less on a twice-a-week basis). As part of the assessment interview preceding assignment to therapy, the patient, in conjunction with the clinician-interviewer, formulates two to three targets, which assumedly become the focus of the subsequent therapy and which are made available to the therapist. Furthermore, changes in the target complaints are hypothesized to be critical indicators of therapeutic change. While our therapists, highly experienced practitioners, are not specifically instructed to gear their treatment efforts to the targets, it is clear to them that the targets are important foci. Nonetheless, it appears that none of the therapists views the targets as central to their therapeutic effort—in fact, they accord them little explicit recognition. These therapists, whom I consider representative of experienced practitioners in the United States, appear to employ a long-term, open-ended model in what they know to be short-term, time-limited psychotherapy. This finding suggests that 1) few therapists are specifically trained to carry out time-limited psychotherapy; and 2) therapists typically view psychotherapy as a unitary process that can only be set in motion but cannot be focused. It is fair to say that the majority of therapists practicing today implicitly, if not explicitly, subscribe to this view, major exceptions being behavior therapists and such authors as Sifneos (1972), and Malan (1963; 1976), who have described and advocated goal-directed approaches in short-term psychotherapy.

It is urgently important that we confront the following questions: *Are short-term goals realistic? With whom, and under what conditions are they viable; that is, what are their limitations? What techniques are optimal to reach specific, or at least reasonably specific, goals? What qualifications and training must the therapist practicing short-term therapy possess to carry out these tasks?*

At present, our ability to answer such questions is woefully inadequate, and the proponents of short-term therapy appear to agree that only a minuscule proportion of the patients coming to an outpatient clinic can be considered suitable candidates. The last stricture is not necessarily a deterrent because it speaks to the issue of what specific treatment, for what specific patients, under what specific conditions.

Proponents of short-term dynamic therapy, in which there is currently considerable interest, have proposed that with suitable patients the therapeutic effort be focused on interpretations dealing with oedipal material (Sifneos, 1972) or on transference interpretations linked to parents (Malan, 1963). It may be true that under appropriate circumstances marked therapeutic benefits can be reaped by these focused approaches; however, despite preliminary evidence presented by these investigators, the question remains open whether alternative approaches may be equally or perhaps more effective; nor can we be certain that the changes resulting from these interventions are indeed a function of the technique to which they are attributed.

I cannot let this opportunity pass without commenting briefly on the importance of the researcher's role in clarifying these issues, and underscoring the indispensability of his work for the advancement of knowledge: Clinicians, on the basis of their understanding and practical experience, propose solutions to practical problems; it remains for the researcher to document whether the *purported* advances are *real* advances. As Cronbach (1975) has cogently observed (p. 126): "The special task of the social scientist in each generation is to pin down the contemporary facts. Beyond that, he shares with the humanistic scholar and the artist [and I would add, the clinician] in the effort to gain insight into contemporary relationships, and to realign the culture's view of man with present realities. To know man as he is is no mean aspiration" (p. 126).

TOWARD A PRODUCTIVE PATIENT-THERAPIST DYAD

While scarcely a revolutionary insight, it is fair to say that psychotherapy is maximally effective when the "right" patient meets the "right" therapist and when the circumstances surrounding their more or less protracted work are "right." Deficiencies in any of these conditions will predictably lessen optimal results and at times vitiate them completely.

With respect to the *patient,* his or her *motivation* to work on important problems in living appears to be increasingly a key factor. In addition, patients considered good prognostic risks are described as:

> young, attractive, well-educated, members of the upper middle class, possessing a high degree of ego strength, some anxiety which impels them to seek help, no seriously disabling neurotic symptoms, relative absence of deep characterological distortions and strong secondary gains, a willingness to talk about their difficulties, an ability to communicate well, some skill in the social-vocational area, and a value system relatively congruent with that of the therapist. Such patients also tend to remain in therapy, profit from it, and evoke the therapist's best efforts. As already noted by superficial behavioristic criteria, such patients may not appear very 'sick'; however, neither our culture nor our psychological tests are very sensitive to unhappiness, silent suffering, and despair (Strupp, 1962, pp. 470-471).

Despite numerous studies published since the time the above was written, little has happened to cause modification of the statement. Nor does it follow, as stated earlier, that psychotherapy is most effective with patients who need it the least. On the other hand, it is true that no patient is an "ideal" candidate; this being the case, appropriate subtractions from an ideal outcome are inevitable.

I have little to add to the subject of propitious *circumstances*—the patient's life situation—which can be a great aid to the therapeutic effort or, alternatively, a great hindrance. Often these impediments prove insuperable, and ideal conditions are rarely encountered. Again, subtractions must be made.

Finally, with respect to the *therapist,* we seem to have come full circle during the last two decades. Freud implied—but never made explicit (except in tangential references) —that the therapist should be a mature, dedicated person who could serve the patient as a model for health identification. In contrast, the therapist's technical contribution (primarily his interpretive skill) came to occupy a position of foremost importance for the outcome of psychotherapy. During the last decade or two, the human-relationship aspects of psychotherapy have come in for more explicit stress in the literature. In fact, some writers have proposed that the therapist's personality is more important than any technique he might use. Some authors (e.g., Rogers, 1957) have gone so far as to question whether technique is important at all (quoted with minor changes from Strupp and Luborsky, 1962). Thus, we had reached a point where the patient and situational factors became relegated to the background, and such variables as the therapist's genuineness, empathy, and unconditional positive regard assumed overriding importance.

More recently, however, serious questions have been raised concerning such a simplistic position. For one thing, a number of studies have failed to support earlier claims that there is a reliable statistical relationship between the aforementioned therapist factors and outcome, and it has generally been recognized that much greater attention must be paid to the dynamics of the patient-therapist relationship, including prominently also the patient factors mentioned earlier. Greater emphasis is again being placed on what the therapist does rather than what he is, but both facets are clearly of crucial importance. Thus the field has moved from an emphasis on technique to an emphasis on the therapist's personality to a position that acknowledges the importance of both, and crucially their interaction.

In this connection should be mentioned the tremendous proliferation of techniques, the large number of persons who have entered the field in therapeutic or quasitherapeutic roles, and the mounting public interest in all aspects of personality growth and psychotherapy. No longer do we have therapists trained in a narrow mold, but the diversity of persons who occupy therapeutic roles, with even greater diversity of backgrounds and training, is truly staggering. As a result, the relationships between therapist's personality and technique and their relative importance in treatment outcomes have become more obscured than they were in the days when analytic training provided rigorous limits to what might be called the therapist's personal participation in the treatment process. While the issue has never been clearly elucidated, the contemporary trend has served to confound it further. We still do not know to what extent a particular treatment outcome is to be credited to the therapist's technical expertise or to personal qualities, which of course interact in any case with his technique.

Theoretical writings and systematic research in this area are not lacking, but clear answers have not been forthcoming. Rogers, long in the forefront of those advocating the therapist's personal qualities, continues to affirm (Rogers, 1975) the overriding importance of such factors as empathy, caring, prizing, and understanding—the last of which he calls "the most precious gift one can give to another" (p. 9). Swenson (1971), after reviewing the literature on the personality of the successful therapist, concludes that the really crucial element in the therapist's contribution to therapeutic success is the therapist's commitment to the client, and he calls for the development of what might be termed a "psychology of commitment." I wholeheartedly concur in this judgment but am less sanguine that commitment can readily be taught to therapists-in-training. Certainly, training experiences which are directly aimed at increasing the level of the therapist's empathy may do no more than enable the trainee to emit verbal messages that receive high ratings on a particular empathy scale. What is also frequently forgotten is that unless the client *experiences* the therapist's empathic understanding and commitment as personally meaningful and authentic, it makes little difference how external raters judge it on a bipolar scale. In short, I believe that the problem is far more complicated than overly optimistic authors and trainers of therapists have suggested; nor is it easy to quantify the essential ingredients that are called for.

There can be little doubt that an empathic and committed therapist is superior to one who is not, but these qualities do not translate into therapeutic success in linear fashion. A problem often arises in that the patient, because of his particular neurotic problems and the totality of his life experience, is incapable of benefiting from these qualities, which more "normal" individuals experience as a genuine therapeutic gift. Indeed, one might go so far as to assert that in some sense the patient's ability to profit from these therapist qualities is proportional to his degree of disturbance. Nevertheless, even a person who has sustained severe trauma and whose ability to trust others has been severely impaired, can identify, and will resonate to, the genuineness of the therapist's empathy and commitment.

In short, caring and commitment are surely crucial ingredients in the therapeutic influence; however, as I have developed elsewhere (Strupp, 1973), I view them as necessary rather than sufficient. Secondly, unless the caring and commitment are genuine, they are worse than useless because the patient will come to see them as counterfeit. Patients have typically had ample exposure to insincerity and dissimulation in human relations, and it is the last thing they need from a therapist. As already mentioned, the literature on "therapist-provided conditions" has taken a far too simplistic view of therapist qualities, and the advocates of training procedures designed to enhance a therapist's empathy have promoted a gimmicky approach which takes scant recognition of the fact that commitment to a profession and to another human being is a quality that grows out of long experience in study and living; it is not available "instantly," nor are there shortcuts to its achievement.

My early research (Strupp, 1960) unexpectedly opened my eyes to an important problem: There appears to be a disturbingly large number of practicing therapists, often highly experienced ones, who have neither the human qualities that would equip them to be of genuine help to another person seeking their professional help with problems in living nor the technical expertise which would enable them to be a truly therapeutic force.

In rejecting the overly simplistic view that therapeutic outcomes are substantially due to "conditions provided by the therapist," which says in effect that neurotic problems melt in the presence of genuineness, empathy, and unconditional positive regard,* I believe that there are certain technical procedures by which the therapist manages to influence the patient's mental structure and/or his behavior for therapeutic gain. For present purposes I am thinking primarily of interpretive techniques, but my point would apply to others as well. There are obviously innumerable ways in which a clarification, an interpretation, a comment on the patient's behavior, etc. can be made. Many of them may be technically "correct," and, assuming a working relationship has been established, they will have a certain therapeutic impact. What, in my judgment, however, is crucial is the *human context* in which they are advanced and how they are *experienced* by the patient. It is the *conjunction of the therapist's personal qualities with his technical skill which at critical points in therapy (but really in all interactions) either engenders a truly corrective emotional experience or fails to do so.* In the latter case, the patient is left defeated, criticized, humiliated, and infantilized; rather than having been corrective, the experience in an important sense may duplicate earlier ones that have played an important part in creating the difficulties from which he is suffering.

The therapist must be capable of understanding the messages that the patient is sending in distorted ways through his associations and his behavior in therapy, and he must be able to decode their meaning. He must understand something about the core of the patient's suffering as well as his contemporary struggles. Again it is a combination of his technical expertise, honed through prolonged training and experience, and his humanity, which permits him to grasp the essential ingredients of the patient's experience and respond to it in truly therapeutic fashion. A therapist who is not committed to the patient as a person, does not care for him, and in a basic sense does not like him cannot accomplish this feat. This is not to say

---

* This view, which gained currency in American psychology largely as a result of client-centered therapy, ignores the complexity of *character*, and along with it the persistence, tenacity, and rigidity of neurotic as well as characterological structures. It substitutes a simple-minded optimism for realities that every clinician has ample opportunity to observe, and it has given rise to the misconception that significant psychotherapeutic change can be obtained from relatively little effort, both from the patient and the therapist. This is not to assert that psychotherapy is futile, but it is only realistic to recognize the forces that typically oppose the therapeutic enterprise.

that a therapist must be all-loving, never irritated, never impatient. Obviously, such paragons do not exist. What is distressing, however, is the observation that relatively few practicing therapists have a fair measure of the human qualities and skills that are indispensable. Even when they are well trained—and regrettably, many therapists practicing today are not—their humanity is often deficient, and it is this lack for which no amount of training, experience, and prolonged practice can compensate. Nor can we readily measure it. But it is as real as anything in human relations and unquestionably the single most important factor in an experience that qualifies as truly therapeutic.

This much is clear: Modern psychotherapy is not, and can never be, the blind application of a set of techniques, but neither is it the untutored influence of a charismatic mentor. It is a unique blending of personal qualities and technical skills that enables the psychotherapist to influence a patient's feelings, cognitions, and life-style for therapeutic purposes. Psychotherapy will perhaps always remain a clinical art, but at its best it is an art in the hands of a highly skilled expert. We may never know precisely how art and science combine in a given person to potentiate his therapeutic influence, and the scientific investigator remains frustrated by the realization that the most important ingredients in the therapist's influence are also the most elusive ones.

REFERENCES

BERGIN, A. E. 1971. The evaluation of therapeutic outcomes. In A. E. Bergin and S. L. Garfield (eds.), *Handbook of Psychotherapy and Behavior Change*, New York: John Wiley & Sons, pp. 217-270.

BRONOWSKI, J. 1973. *The Ascent of Man*. Boston: Little, Brown.

CRONBACH, L. J. 1974. Beyond the two disciplines of scientific psychology. *American Psychologist*, 30:116-127.

EYSENCK, H. J. 1952. The effects of psychotherapy: An evaluation. *Journal of Consulting Psychology*, 16:319-324.

FREUD, S. 1933. New introductory lectures. *The Standard Edition of the Complete Psychological Works of Sigmund Freud*, Vol. 22. London: Hogarth Press, 1964, pp. 136-157.

FREUD, S. 1937. Analysis terminable and interminable. *The Standard Edition of the Complete Psychological Works of Sigmund Freud*, Vol. 23. London: Hogarth Press, 1964, pp. 211-253.

KIESLER, D. J. 1966. Some myths of psychotherapy research and the search for a paradigm. *Psychol. Bull.* 65:110-136.

LUBORSKY, L. and STRUPP, H. H. 1962. Research problems in psychotherapy: A three-year follow-up. In H. H. Strupp and L. Luborsky (eds.), *Research in Psychotherapy,* Vol. 2. Washington, D.C.: American Psychological Association, pp. 308-329.

MALAN, D. H. 1963. *A Study in Brief Psychotherapy.* Springfield, Ill.: Charles C Thomas.

MALAN, D. H. 1976. *Towards the Validation of Dynamic Psychotherapy.* New York: Plenum.

ROGERS, C. R. 1957. The necessary and sufficient conditions of therapeutic personality change. *Journal of Consulting Psychology.* 22:95-103.

ROGERS, C. R. 1975. Empathic: An unappreciated way of being. *Counseling Psychologist* 5 (2):2-10.

SIFNEOS, P. E. 1972. *Short-Term Psychotherapy and Emotional Crisis.* Cambridge, Mass.: Harvard University Press.

STRUPP, H. H. 1960. *Psychotherapists in Action: Explorations of the Therapist's Contribution to the Treatment Process.* New York: Grune & Stratton.

STRUPP, H. H. 1962. Psychotherapy. In P. R. Farnsworth (ed.), *Annual Review of Psychology,* Vol. 13. Palo Alto, Cal.: Annual Reviews, pp. 445-478.

STRUPP, H. H. 1973. Toward a reformulation of the psychotherapeutic influence. *Int. J. Psychiatry,* 11:263-265.

STRUPP, H. H. and BERGIN, A. E. 1969. Some empirical and conceptual bases for co-ordinated research in psychotherapy: A critical review of issues, trends, and evidence. *Int. J. Psychiatry,* 7:18-90.

STRUPP, H. H. and LUBORSKY, L. (eds.) 1962. *Research in Psychotherapy.* Vol. 2. Washington, D.C.: American Psychological Association.

SWENSON, C. H. 1971. Commitment and the personality of the successful therapist. *Psychotherapy: Theory, Research and Practice,* 8:31-36.

2

Psychotherapy and Pharmacotherapy of Schizophrenia

PHILIP R. A. MAY, M.D.

There are still a lingering few who believe that drugs have no place in the treatment of schizophrenia, and that they are incompatible with dynamically oriented psychotherapy and psychosocial methods. This resistance is, however, rapidly passing into history. When drugs were first introduced, dire predictions were rampant (Klerman, 1963). Medications would focus attention on symptoms rather than cause; they would increase magical reliance on the physician and foster dependency. The patient's capacity for insight would be blunted, and recovery would be impossible. Drugs would also have harmful effects on the psychiatrist by inducing him to seek an easy way out. Thus irrational motives and authoritarian trends were attributed to those who prescribed drugs. (Apparently it was assumed that those who did not do so were entirely immune to such human weaknesses.) Alarm was even expressed over the moral consequences for the nation as a whole.

This opposition to drugs came largely from places that had pinned their hopes on intensive use of some other form of treatment, mostly psychotherapy or milieu therapy. In these settings drugs were used with little discretion, in small doses (Hordern, 1961), and with little

---

The ratings of Design-Relevance used in this paper were made by Dr. Theodore Van Putten (Veterans Administration Hospital, Brentwood, California; assistant professor of psychiatry in residence, University of California at Los Angeles) and the author, as described in May and Van Putten, 1974. They were based on detailed abstracts published in a previous review (May, 1975).

understanding of their side effects (Klerman, 1963). Perhaps we should not be surprised that there is resistance to the impact of research on clinical practice. This resistance is plainly a matter of general concern, not specific to psychiatry; it is not even specific to medicine. Max Planck in his autobiography (1971) referred to the bitter struggles over his new models of the structure of matter. He observed sardonically, "A new scientific truth does not triumph by convincing its opponents and making them see the light but rather because its opponents eventually die, and a new generation grows up that is familiar with it."

So also in the treatment of schizophrenia. Times have changed. We have come slowly and painfully to recognize that we do not yet know the certain "cause" of schizophrenia, that symptomatic improvement cannot be detached from other modes of improvement, and that insight is neither necessary nor sufficient for restitution. Now, some 20 years after the introduction of chlorpromazine, we have a new generation more experienced in pharmacotherapy. It is almost universally held that drugs, psychotherapy, and psychosocial methods should play supplemental rather than competing roles. The general opinion is that drugs have their greatest use in restoring contact and establishing therapeutic relationships in the stage of flagrant psychosis. Once perceptual control has been reestablished and secondary symptoms have been reduced, and once the patient is in better contact and a relationship has been formed, then these other psychological and social methods can work better toward mastery of personality difficulties, life problems, and behavioral incapacities.

As a final comment in this brief review of history, I have never been entirely able to understand why Freud's views on the possibilities of psychopharmacology have been generally ignored. Indeed, as Byck (1974) points out, Freud should be considered one of the founders and pioneers of psychopharmacology. He introduced a systematic scientific methodology into the study of centrally active drugs, and considered in his papers a number of points that have become major issues in modern psychopharmacology.

In 1914 Freud wrote: ". . . we must recollect that all . . . provisional ideas in psychology will presumably some day be based on an organic substructure. This makes it probable that it is special substances and chemical processes which perform the operations of . . . special psychical forces."

In 1930 he wrote: "The hope of the future here lies in organic chemistry or access to it through endocrinology. This future is still far distant but one should study analytically every case of psychosis because this knowledge will one day guide the chemical therapy."

In 1933 Freud took the position that psychoanalysis did not stand in opposition to other therapeutic methods, diminish their value, or exclude them. He also expressed the hope that hormones might eventually provide us with a successful means of coping with the maldistribution of energy in the psychoses.

In 1938 he wrote: ". . . we are concerned with therapy only insofar as it works by psychological means, and for the time being we have no other. The future may teach us to exercise a direct influence, by means of particular chemical substances, on the amounts of energy and their distribution in the neural apparatus. It may be that there are other undreamt-of possibilities of therapy. But for the moment we have nothing better at our disposal than the techniques of psychoanalysis. . . ."

Terminology

A great deal of confusion has been caused by the failure to make a few important distinctions among terms. *Psychotherapy* may be defined as a deliberate attempt to focus on the patient's sensitivities to life experiences, and through understanding and discussion to strengthen his ability to gain mastery of his situation. As such, it must be distinguished from the basic *therapeutic relationship* that is essential to success with any kind of treatment, be it surgical, medical or social.

If psychotherapy is defined as above, then other psychological and psychosocial approaches to treatment such as social casework, milieu therapy, occupational therapy, and rehabilitation can be included under the rubric of *psychotherapeutic management* (May, 1968a).

Review of Controlled Studies

Psychotherapy and psychotherapeutic management are expensive commodities; it is important, therefore, to know whether drugs potentiate or interfere with their effects. Which treatment gets better results, in which type of case? Is one treatment more useful at some particular stage of the illness, or for some particular purpose?

In general, this subject has been sadly troubled by dogmatic expressions of opinion, and—with a few prominent exceptions—a dearth of well controlled experimental evidence. Personally I prefer systematic observation. I like to know when I am operating on faith and hope, rather than on the basis of scientific evidence. Yet a poorly controlled study can, of course, be just as misleading as a report of a single case. Accordingly, the controlled studies examined here will be classified by the degree of confidence with which their findings can be applied to the treatment of schizophrenia.

METHODOLOGY

All controlled studies of nonpharmacologic therapeutic outcome reported up to mid-1973 (May, 1975) were classified* and rated on the Design-Relevance (D-R) Scale (May and Van Putten, 1974).

The findings were tabulated for all prospective studies with six or more schizophrenic patients who had been treated in the same facility and had served as a control group (i.e., Categories I through IV of the Design-Relevance Scale**). Ratings were also assigned to the comparable studies of pharmacologic treatment surveyed by Cole and Davis (1969). (The findings from their review are so definite that additional material on drug therapy beyond 1968 is unnecessary.)

Through this tabulation and assignment of ratings it is possible to assess the weight of the evidence. The sum of the Design-Relevance ratings of studies that found no benefit (or worse) is subtracted from the sum for studies that reported positive results. The net result is an estimate of the strength of the supporting evidence. Studies with doubtful or questionable positive findings are excluded, that is, they

---

* A study by Honigfeld, Rosenblum, Blumenthal, Lambert, and Roberts (1965) was excluded because the findings may be relevant only for geriatric schizophrenic patients.
** On the D-R scale, studies in Category I (well executed, well designed, and well analyzed) are given between 84 and 96 points, depending on the number of patients studied and the breadth of the assessment of patient change. Studies in Category IV, the lowest included in this review, are given 24 to 36 points.

TABLE 1

Milieu Care and Rehabilitation—Controlled Studies to 1973, Questionable or Doubtful Positive Evidence Excluded

Comparison	D-R Points
Inpatient milieu care better than control	+259
Outpatient aftercare better than control	+369
Daycare or home treatment equal to or better than inpatient care	+150

are counted as neither for nor against the hypothesis of treatment effect.

WEIGHT OF EVIDENCE

Milieu Care and Rehabilitation

Table 1 summarizes the evidence on milieu care and rehabilitation. There is reasonably good evidence that inpatient milieu treatment programs produce beneficial results (259 D-R points). The programs that were effective concentrated on real-life problems and on planning for discharge; there is little evidence that other types of in-hospital milieu programs are effective in the treatment of schizophrenic patients.

On the other hand, there is reasonable evidence (150 D-R points) that day care or home care, when practical, is as good as or even better than inpatient treatment, provided that drug treatment is adequately given. There is also adequate evidence (369 D-R points) that aftercare programs improve the results by helping the patient to remain in the community after discharge from hospital. The successful programs focused mainly on problem-solving, social adjustment, living arrangements, employment, and facilitating cooperation with maintenance drug therapy.

Psychotherapy

Table 2 summarizes the data on psychotherapy. The breakdown of inpatient vs. outpatient and type of therapy are illuminating. The balance of the evidence suggests that inpatients treated with

Table 2

Psychotherapy—Controlled Studies to 1973, Questionable or Doubtful Positive Evidence Excluded

	Comparison	D-R Points
A. Inpatient psychotherapy	Individual better than control	—192
	Group (standard) better than control	—51
	Group (reality-activity) better than control	+100
	Group (reality-activity) better than standard	+51
B. Outpatient psychotherapy	Individual casework and rehabilitation better than control	+90
	Group therapy better than control	+31
	Group therapy better than individual	+64

individual psychotherapy or standard group therapy did not improve more than a control group *(minus* 192 and *minus* 51 D-R points respectively). By contrast, inpatient group therapy that is deliberately not aimed at psychological understanding is somewhat more encouraging. Group therapy that centered around reality or a group activity was more effective than control (100 D-R points) and standard group therapy (51 D-R points).

Studies on outpatient psychotherapy are few and far between, but they support the view that psychotherapy (especially group therapy) is helpful with outpatients (90 D-R points favor individual casework and rehabilitation over control; 31 D-R points favor group therapy over control and 64 D-R points favor group therapy over individual). Positive results were obtained particularly when treatment focused on social and occupational rehabilitation, problem-solving, and cooperation with pharmacotherapy; that is, more success was obtained when treatment was oriented toward support and rehabilitation rather than formal attempts to promote insight and deeper psychological understanding.

This interpretation of the controlled findings up to mid-1973 is supported by a recent controlled study of outpatient psychotherapy combined with drug therapy (Claghorn et al., 1974). This investigation found that group therapy which was structured to emphasize the problems and tasks of daily living in combination with maintenance drug treaatment resulted in a statistically significant shift

TABLE 3

Other Treatment—Controlled Studies to 1973, Questionable or Doubtful Positive Evidence Excluded

Comparison	D-R Points
Nicotinic acid better than control	—302
ECT better than control	—205
Phenothiazine more effective than ECT	+100
Behavioral conditioning better than control	+25
Behavioral conditioning better than group therapy	—29
Antipsychotic drugs better than control	+7,080*

* Data to 1968 only. Estimated from Cole and Davis, 1969.

toward patients' "healthier" (mostly self-reported) perceptions of themselves and of others. (This shift was not accompanied, however, by any changes in clinical ratings.)

Other Forms of Treatment

Table 3 shows that the greatest evidence of therapeutic effect has been obtained for antipsychotic drug therapy (many thousands of D-R points). The evidence is negative for nicotinic acid and electroconvulsive therapy (ECT) (*minus* 302 and *minus* 205 D-R points, respectively). Behavioral conditioning is virtually untested by controlled studies (25 D-R points suggest that it is better than control, 29 points that it is less effective than group therapy).

The evidence in favor of pharmacotherapy is overwhelming. This should not prevent us from recognizing, however, that drugs alone are unlikely to be sufficient for an optimal result. Psychosocial interventions may be of crucial importance, particularly in chronic cases and when there is residual disability. Granted, there is only modest evidence (116 D-R points) that inpatient milieu and group psychotherapy programs are of benefit, and then largely when they center on some kind of activity or focus on discharge planning and social and occupational rehabilitation. There is, however, four times as much evidence (490 D-R points) in favor of outpatient care along similar lines; in fact, day care or home care, when feasible, produced better results than inpatient care (150 D-R points). Thus there is considerable evidence to underline the value of combining pharmacotherapy with outpatient efforts to reduce residual disability after remission of the acute psychosis, and to develop and promote social and occupational skills.

The evidence seems small beside the massive weight of controlled research in drug therapy, but it is consistent and positive. Perhaps if there were more well designed studies, the disproportion in weight vis-à-vis drug therapy might be reduced. Unfortunately, practitioners of social, occupational, and psychotherapeutic rehabilitation have, in general, been extremely reluctant to participate in controlled studies of high quality. I am skeptical of the customary excuse that such research is particularly difficult. A number of studies (e.g., Greenblatt et al., 1965; Fairweather et al., 1969; Caffey, Galbrecht, and Klett, 1971; Meltzoff and Blumenthal, 1966; Hogarty and Goldberg, 1973; and Claghorn et al., 1974) have demonstrated that it is entirely feasible.

DO ANTIPSYCHOTIC DRUGS INTERFERE WITH PSYCHOTHERAPY AND SOCIOTHERAPY?

The controlled studies of treatment outcome reviewed by Uhlenhuth, Lipman and Covi (1969) and May (1968b, 1971) indicate that drug and other treatments generally do not interfere with one another. According to the criterion of the ultimate outcome of cases followed from admission, the combination of drugs and psychosocial therapy is quite clearly superior to psychotherapy and sociotherapy alone. There is, however, no doubt that drugs, especially in large doses, may produce troublesome side effects that work against psychological and social therapy.

The difficulty is that the hard-core experimentalists focus on main effects, and on data and statistics for outcome from admission across all patients, while their opposition focuses on toxic effects, on individual patients who did not do well on drugs, or on patients who are drug-resistant or who may do better when taken off drugs. It seems to me that both groups are right, but each grasps only part of the elephant.

There is a trade-off between the beneficial antipsychotic effects of a drug and its adverse side effects. The optimum trade-off point varies from patient to patient and according to the immediate goals of treatment at any particular time. When patients are "snowed" with drugs, obviously they cannot benefit from social or psychological treatment (Appleton, 1965). There is also no doubt that some patients are continued on drug treatment too long, or at higher dosage than is optimal (Paul, Tobias, and Holly, 1972). The skill in drug therapy is to avoid large doses, except in the early stages of treatment or in unusual situations, and to monitor the process of treatment closely so that dosage can be adjusted to the trade-off point that is optimal for the current goals of treatment. In general, the closer the patient comes to "normal," the more we should be careful to reduce drug dosage to the minimum required for maintenance of perceptual control.

THE NATURE OF DRUG EFFECT

It is commonly asserted that drug therapy acts only to reduce anxiety and is "superficial" or "only supportive." This is not in line with the evidence from controlled studies which shows that drugs affect the primary symptoms of schizophrenia more than the secondary ones (Cole and Davis, 1969). The implication is that antipsychotic drugs reduce psychotic distortions of reality and so reduce the anxiety that is secondary to those distortions.

It is, of course, reasonable to assume that lifetime patterns are not easily modified, and to be suspicious of any suggestion that short-term treatment of any kind can promote radical change. But there is virtually no information available about change at "deeper" levels over a prolonged period on *any* type of therapy, and certainly no experimental support for the notion that more of such change occurs during psychosocial treatments than during an equivalent period of drug therapy.

On the other side of the fence, there is no hard evidence that psychological and social treatments are more than palliative; they help some persons to make the best use of their resources, rather than actually remedying the primary disorder, whatever it may be.

Therapeutic Relationships and Psychopharmacotherapy

It is sometimes, even frequently, assumed that drug treatment requires no particular skill and no particular attention to the transactions of the therapeutic relationship. This is a serious error. The effectiveness of *any* kind of treatment depends on a good relationship with the patient and his family, and the vicissitudes of these relationships have a profound impact on the course of pharmacotherapy. *Establishing a continuing positive relationship must therefore occupy a central position in the overall strategy for treating the schizophrenic patient, whatever the form of treatment employed.*

Patients have preformed ideas of what treatment to expect, and judicious pharmacotherapy must take account of the significance that drug prescribing and taking has for a particular patient, his perception of the total situation, and the motives he ascribes to the person giving the drug. A patient's negative attitudes toward medication may reflect attitudes to the physician, or to his family. There is, in effect, negative and positive transference to a drug, which is just as irrational as transference to the psychotherapist. For example, the control of symptoms that signify impulsivity and ego weakness to the patient may have an immediate ego-fortifying effect. Less favorable results may be expected if the patient interprets drug effect as threatening his own controls or as mind control or hostile rejection, or if drug-induced lassitude awakens fears of passivity or physical harm (Sarwer-Foner, 1960, 1963).

Transference

Fears have been expressed that drugs may distort the transference. The transference of the psychotic patient is distorted in any case, however, and the essential point is to confront fantasy with reality. The conscious and unconscious meanings of medication and its mechanics can be analyzed just as readily as the conscious and unconscious meanings of psychotherapy and the arrangements for payment, therapeutic parameters, and so forth. Nevertheless, pharmacotherapy affords rapid relief from pain, and there is the possibility that the pharmacotherapist could be aggrandized and credited with magic. (Magical expectations are not, of course, confined to pharmacotherapy. I suspect that the incidence of magical expectations depends more on the prejudices of the patient and the charisma and style of the therapist than on the method employed, be it drug therapy, psychotherapy, therapeutic-community, or behavior therapy. I am not aware of any controlled studies in this area.)

Countertransference

Pharmacotherapy may be employed for nonrational countertransference reasons, to keep distance from a patient (Sarwer-Foner, 1960), or because the therapist feels inadequate (Lesse, 1956). There are equally irrational reasons for *not* giving drugs, such as the narcissism and rescue fantasies of therapists who want to cure the patient all by themselves (Rickels, 1962). Some of us have a puritanical prejudice against using drugs to obtain relief, subscribing to the moralistic idea that psychological suffering is different from physical pain: a person must work his way out and not get relief too easily (Ostow, 1966).

Divergent attitudes toward pharmacotherapy may also be a manifestation of conflicts between professions and ideologies. For example, social workers and others who specialize in psychotherapy and social intervention may react to drugs as a threat to their professional status (Klerman, 1960). Community mental health centers commonly attract staff members whose opposition to pharmacotherapy is fundamentally ideological (Schulberg and Baker, 1975).

Social Class

Treatment for lower-class psychotic patients is often biased toward physical forms of treatment (Shader, Binstock, and Scott, 1968; Carlson et al., 1965). Admittedly they are often uninterested in psychotherapy and, according to reported studies, regard it as less important than recreation and rehabilitation. However, it would be unwise to assume that pharmacotherapy is more appropriate in such patients, since they also tend to be suspicious of medication, and denigrate and cooperate poorly with it.

Limitations of Drug Therapy

Drugs have their limitations. They can never be all there is to the treatment of the schizophrenic person; they may be helpful in promoting restitution, but they sometimes have toxic effects. Moreover, they do not enlighten the patient about his problems, inform him how to adapt, help him to take advantage of opportunities, nor accept his limitations. They do not repair self-esteem, nor do they repair the damage he has done to his friends and family. They cannot get him a job; they cannot make mothers or mothers-in-law change their minds; they do not handle traffic violations, and they cannot teach him to do something he could not do before. Obviously, therefore, treatment must include intervention by someone who has a relationship with the schizophrenic person and who tries to help him with the practical affairs of everyday living.

Limitations of Milieu Treatment

Milieu therapy can also have toxic, antitherapeutic effects, particularly when techniques and methods developed for neurotics and character disorders are indiscriminately applied to psychotic patients. For patients who have defects in perception, attention, and information processing, or who are disorganized and hyperaroused, the typical "milieu ward" with its high stimulus input, lively group meetings, role diffusion, searches for hidden meanings, loud music, and inability to distinguish staff from patients by dress, may constitute a toxic dose of environmental stimulation (Van Putten, 1973). Delayed toxic effects may also occur. Patients tend to conform to an institutional culture, whatever it may be, but what happens when patients adjust to a hospital society that is radically different from the outside world?

The introduction of drug therapy prompts a reappraisal. There are still a number of hard-core, treatment-resistant patients, for whom inpatient milieu care may be beneficial. But, with the use of modern psychotropic drugs the hospital is, for the average schizophrenic patient, essentially a center for relatively brief crisis treatment. New social patterns and techniques should not be sought at the added cost of prolonged hospitalization, which deprives the patient of the potentially sustaining and satisfying ego-organizing influence of work, family, and friends. The emphasis should shift from indiscriminate application of the cumbersome, time-consuming, and expensive milieu methods of yesterday toward specific interventions to expedite restitution and to prepare the patient and his family for outpatient aftercare and rehabilitation.

The greatest potential lies in a shift toward outpatient treatment. Milieu therapy has usually been conceptualized as a purely intra-hospital affair, dichotomized from outpatient care and estranged or divorced from posthospital aftercare and rehabilitation. In my opinion, this constricted four-walls approach should be replaced by an "expanded-milieu" concept. Physicians, nurses, social workers, psychologists, and rehabilitation therapists should provide genuine continuity of care, and develop techniques and approaches for an extramural milieu therapy that thoughtfully integrates occupational and social rehabilitation.

LIMITATIONS OF PSYCHOTHERAPY

Regardless of the therapist's skill, psychotherapy is often unable to overcome opposing influences in the environment, and there are practical limitations of cost and availability of therapists who are willing to work with schizophrenic patients. Psychotherapy has toxic effects, too. It can make some patients worse, especially when there is a negative transference or a serious countertransference. Destructive acting-out may occur when inhibitions are lifted, and some patients protract therapy indefinitely and become chronically dependent on their therapist (Ostow, 1961). Sexual involvement with the therapist is a potential toxic effect.

DEPENDENCY

Patients may also come to depend on drugs. The major ataraxics do not induce physical dependence, however, and they are not perceived as pleasure-producing: There have been no reports of addiction. The dependency I refer to is of an altogether different type. Dependency may occur because the patient reacts not only to the pill, but to the physician prescribing it and to the context in which it is administered. Thus it is hard to distinguish dependence on *drugs* from dependence on the *therapist* and on *psychotherapy*. Indeed, they are all facets of dependence on the patient-therapist relationship.

DEFINING TREATMENT GOALS

There is, as yet, no universally effective and lasting cure for schizophrenia. Many patients regain their premorbid level of functioning. But re-ordering a pathological style of personality functioning is a difficult if not impossible task to achieve by the methods currently available. Hence, a major point of strategy: defining goals for each patient. It is important to distinguish between trying to achieve or maintain restitution, and trying to remake the patient. It is important also to remember that what is good for one patient may not be good for another; what helps in the early stages of treatment may not help at all later on; and measures aimed, for example, toward getting the patient a job may have no effect on his temper tantrums. It is therefore essential to define clearly what the goals are and to plan specific treatment accordingly. The days when we prescribed a rodomontade of drug therapy, occupational therapy, recreational therapy, milieu therapy, a therapeutic community, and so forth for everyone should be gone forever. We hope that new methods of problem-oriented and goal-oriented record-keeping will prod us in this direction.

Ignorance of psychopharmacology, unnecessary use of drugs, lack of psychotherapeutic skill, and scotomata for sociotherapy, family therapy, and rehabilitation are all equally inexcusable.

INTEGRATION

The task is to integrate pharmacotherapy with other forms of treatment, and to tailor a treatment plan for the individual patient. Although, on the whole, drugs are likely to give better results at less cost than do other treatments, this does not mean that everyone should be given drugs indiscriminately. Patients who are already on the way to restitution should not be given drugs unless there is a good possibility that medication will improve their final condition or lessen their financial burden. Equally so, drugs should not be continued forever in those who fail to respond to adequate doses.

These cautionary remarks must be accompanied by a similar admonition that psychotherapy and social forms of intervention should be used with equal discrimination. Judging by the results of controlled research, the value of psychotherapy and milieu therapy for inpatients has been greatly exaggerated. It helps to focus on practical matters such as getting a person a job or a place to live, or improving his social skills, but there are more prudent ways of spending resources: for example, working with other members of the family, or saving the money to provide better care and rehabilitation after the patient leaves the hospital. We must constantly keep in mind that ivory-tower treatment of the patient, apart from his social and family context, is less likely to succeed than thoughtful involvement of those others who may be significant in his life.

One aspect of family treatment that has been singularly neglected is the effect of schizophrenic patients on their children. Preventive and remedial work with this high-risk group could be most rewarding. Just as the child psychiatrist routinely interviews and works with parents, so should the psychiatrist or some member of his treatment team work with the children of adult patients. It is impressive to see what is added to the understanding and treatment of the schizophrenic patient when this is done.

CONCLUSION: PROGRAM DEVELOPMENT

As we have seen, the evidence indicates that psychosocial interventions are likely to be of most help in the outpatient phase. The overall treatment strategy should therefore center on a vigorous effort to provide continuity of follow-up and aftercare, and to integrate drug therapy, psychotherapy, casework management, and rehabilitation. Yet the unfortunate facts are that, with a very few outstanding exceptions, hospitals continue to initiate relationships that are terminated on discharge. Patients are rarely looked after by the same treatment team in and out of the hospital, and the bulk of the effort is still concentrated precisely where controlled research has shown the least evidence of effectiveness. To be cost-effective, the manpower available should be channeled into providing genuine continuity of care by the same treatment team and into keeping the patient out of the hospital rather than keeping him in.

Our pharmacotherapy is equally in need of improvement. At present, expert pharmacotherapy is uncommon in or out of the hospital, and continuity of drug treatment after the patient leaves the hospital is only beginning to become available.

Humility and realistic exploration are in order. There are three fundamental approaches to the treatment of schizophrenia: 1) physical-biological; 2) personal-psychological; and 3) social-occupational. Each is necessary, but in itself insufficient.

Two overall guidelines will help to keep us on the track. First, Freud's prediction (1930), cited above, that psychological understanding will be useful, indeed essential, in monitoring and guiding the course of chemical therapy. Second, Eugen Bleuler's observation that the treatment of schizophrenia is most rewarding, particularly for the physician who does not ascribe the results of natural healing to his own intervention. Yet his cardinal rule was:

> No patient must ever be completely given up; the doctor must always be prepared to take action and to offer the patient the chance to abandon his pathological way of thinking (1911).

Further research will doubtless improve our understanding and our therapeutic techniques. But our treatment planning should center on reality. The effectiveness of treatment programs for the schizophrenic patient could be vastly improved if we were simply to apply the knowledge that we now have.

SUMMARY

This paper examines the implications for treatment planning that can be derived from the findings of controlled studies of pharmacotherapy and psychotherapy in schizophrenia. Its findings should not be generalized to the treatment of other disorders.

There is considerable evidence to emphasize the importance of combining drug therapy with outpatient psychotherapy, psychotherapeutic management, and psychosocial programs. The evidence strongly suggests also that psychotherapeutic intervention in schizophrenia should be goal-directed and aimed particularly at developing and promoting social and occupational skills and at eliciting cooperation with appropriate drug treatment, and monitoring its progress.

Unfortunately, in the past much treatment effort has been concentrated precisely where controlled research has shown the least positive evidence of effectiveness. It would be more likely to be cost-effective if the manpower available were to be channeled into providing genuine continuity of care by the same treatment team, and into efforts to coordinate psychotherapeutic and psychosocial interventions with a system to provide and monitor continuing and truly adequate drug therapy.

Some of the factors that are important in the interface between pharmacotherapy, psychotherapy, and psychosocial strategies are discussed. It is concluded that the effectiveness of treatment programs for the schizophrenic patient could be vastly improved if we were simply to apply the knowledge that we now have.

REFERENCES

APPLETON, W. S. 1965. The snow phenomenon: Tranquilizing the assaultive. *Psychiatry*, 28:88-93.

BLEULER, E. 1911. *Dementia Praecox or the Group of Schizophrenias* (1950). New York: International Universities Press.

BYCK, J. (ed.), 1974. *Cocaine Papers by Sigmund Freud*. New York: Stonehill.

CAFFEY, E. M., JR., GALBRECHT, C. R., and KLETT, C. J. 1971. Brief hospitalization and aftercare in the treatment of schizophrenia. *Arch. Gen. Psychiatry*, 24:81-86.

CARLSON, D. A., COLEMAN, J. V., ERRERA, P., and HARRISON, R. W. 1965. Problems in treating the lower-class psychotic. *Arch. Gen. Psychiatry*, 13:269-274.

CLAGHORN, J. L., JOHNSTONE, E. E., COOK, T. H., and ITSCHNER, L. 1974. Group therapy and maintenance treatment of schizophrenics. *Arch. Gen. Psychiatry*, 31:361-365.

COLE, J. O. and DAVIS, J. M. 1969. Antipsychotic drugs. In L. Bellak and L. Loeb (eds.), *The Schizophrenic Syndrome*. New York: Grune & Stratton, pp. 478-568.

FAIRWEATHER, G. W., SANDERS, D. H., CRESSLER, D. L., and MAYNARD, H. 1969. *Community Life for the Mentally Ill*. Chicago: Aldine.

FREUD, S. 1914. On narcissism—an introduction (1962). *The Complete Psychological Works of Sigmund Freud*. J. Strachey (trans.), Vol. 14. London: Hogarth Press, p. 73.

FREUD, S. 1930. Letter to Marie Bonaparte, January 15, 1930. Cited by E. Jones (1957) in *The Life and Work of Sigmund Freud*. Vol. 3. New York: Basic Books, p. 449.

FREUD, S. 1933. New Introductory Lectures on Psychoanalysis (1964). *The Complete Psychological Works of Sigmund Freud*. J. Strachey (trans.), Vol. 22. London: Hogarth Press, p. 136.

FREUD, S. 1938. An Outline of Psychoanalysis (1964). *The Complete Psychological Works of Sigmund Freud.* J. Strachey (trans.), Vol. 23. London: Hogarth Press, p. 172.

GREENBLATT, M., SOLOMON, H. C., EVANS, A. S., and BROOKS, G. W. (eds.) 1965. *Drugs and Social Therapy in Chronic Schizophrenia.* Springfield, Ill.: Charles C Thomas.

HOGARTY, G. E. and GOLDBERG, S. C. 1973. Drugs and sociotherapy in the post-hospital maintenance of schizophrenic patients: One year relapse rates. *Arch. Gen. Psychiatry,* 28:54-64.

HONIGFELD, G., ROSENBLUM, M. P., BLUMENTHAL, I. J., LAMBERT, H. L., and ROBERTS, A. J. 1965. Behavioral improvement in the older schizophrenic patient: Drug and social therapies. *J. Am. Geriatr. Soc.,* 13:57-72.

HORDERN, A. 1961. Psychiatry and the tranquilizers. *N. Engl. J. Med.,* 265:584-588 and 634-638.

KLERMAN, G. L. 1960. Staff attitudes, decision-making and the use of drug therapy in the mental hospital. In H. C. B. Denber (comp. and ed.), *Research Conference on Therapeutic Community.* Springfield, Ill.: Charles C Thomas, pp. 191-210.

KLERMAN, G. L. 1963. Assessing the influence of the hospital milieu upon the effectiveness of psychiatric drug therapy: Problems of conceptualization and of research methodology. *J. Nerv. Ment. Dis.,* 137:143-154.

LESSE, S. 1956. Psychotherapy and ataraxics. *Am. J. Psychother.,* 10:448-459.

MAY, P. R. A. 1968a. *Treatment of Schizophrenia.* New York: Science House.

MAY, P. R. A. 1968b. Antipsychotic drugs and other forms of therapy. In D. H. Efron, J. O. Cole, J. Levine, and J. B. Wittenborn (eds.), *Psychopharmacology—Review of Progress, 1957-1967.* Public Health Service Publication 1836. Washington, D.C.: U.S. Gov. Printing Office, pp. 1155-1176.

MAY, P. R. A. 1971. Psychotherapy and ataraxic drugs. In A. E. Bergin and S. L. Garfield (eds.), *Handbook of Psychotherapy and Behavior Change.* New York: John Wiley & Sons, pp. 495-540.

MAY, P. R. A. 1975. Schizophrenia: Evaluation of treatment methods. In A. M. Freedman, H. I. Kaplan, and B. J. Sadock (eds.), *Comprehensive Textbook of Psychiatry—II,* Baltimore: Williams & Wilkins, pp. 955-982.

MAY, P. R. A. and VAN PUTTEN, T. 1974. Treatment of schizophrenia: II. A proposed rating scale of design and outcome for use in literature surveys. *Compr. Psychiatry,* 15:267-275.

MELTZOFF, J. and BLUMENTHAL, R. 1966. *The Day Treatment Center.* Springfield, Ill.: Charles C Thomas.

OSTOW, M. 1961. The advantages and limitations of combined therapy. *Psychosomatics,* 2:11-15.

OSTOW, M. 1966. Continuing drug needs in mental illness and its pathogenetic use. In *Symposium: Non-narcotic Drug Dependency and Addiction.* New York County District Branch, American Psychiatric Association.

PAUL, G. L., TOBIAS L. L., and HOLLY, B. L. 1972. Maintenance psychotropic drugs in the presence of active treatment programs. *Arch. Gen. Psychiatry,* 27:106-115.

PLANCK, M. 1971 (repr. ed.). *Scientific Autobiography and Other Papers.* Westport, Conn.: Greenwood Press.

RICKELS, K. 1962. Discussion of Baumgartner, E. I. "Psychotherapy and drugs in general practice." In J. H. Nodine and J. H. Moyer (eds.), *Psychosomatic Medicine.* Philadelphia: Lea & Febiger, p. 801.

SARWER-FONER, G. J. 1960. The role of neuroleptic medication in psychotherapeutic interaction. *Compr. Psychiatry,* 1:291-300.

SARWER-FONER, G. 1963. On the mechanisms of action of neuroleptic drugs: A theoretical psychodynamic explanation. *Recent Advances in Biological Psychiatry,* 6:217-232.

SCHULBERG, H. C. and BAKER, F. 1975. *The Mental Hospital & Human Services.* New York: Behavioral Publications.

SHADER, R. I., BINSTOCK, W. A., and SCOTT, D. 1968. Subjective determinants of drug prescription. A study of therapists' attitudes. *Hosp. Community Psychiatry,* 19: 384-387.

UHLENHUTH, E. H., LIPMAN, R. S., and COVI, L. 1969. Combined pharmacotherapy and psychotherapy: Controlled studies. *J. Nerv. Ment. Dis.,* 148:52-64.

VAN PUTTEN, T. 1973. Milieu therapy: Contraindications? *Arch. Gen. Psychiatry,* 29: 640-643.

3

The Hazards of Treatment and How to Deal with Them

GEORGE M. SIMPSON, M.B., CH.B.

The hazards of treatment in psychiatry, as in other fields, arise from insufficient available information and insufficient use of the already existing knowledge.

It may seem inappropriate but I believe it is germane to begin with a discussion of the legal aspects of treatment since these have received much attention recently. They involve the right to treatment of the patient, but from the point of view of this paper, I would like to focus on the right to no treatment (the hazards of no treatment) which is becoming an increasing problem. If we assume that there exists a type of schizophrenia that is chronic, progressive, generally downhill, producing a disturbance in personality and social function, that is, resulting in a schizophrenic defect, then the person who is quietly psychotic, perhaps harming no one, who does not want treatment and under new regulations is not committable, presents a formidable problem.

I mention this issue here in relation to patients who were obviously psychotic and had been so for one, two, or more years, resulting in a disastrous home situation and tremendous amounts of frustration and guilt in all the family members. There was no way of getting these persons to see a psychiatrist voluntarily, nor was there a psychiatrist who would do a visit under these circumstances; even if one had, these persons would not have been committable within the meaning of the law. This situation often leads the sick individual to lose contact with family members. In one fortunate case, a situation was contrived in which the patient saw a physician and was given an injection of a long-acting drug. Her psychotic symptoms quickly disappeared, producing a total change in the family constellation. With increasing emphasis on treatment in the community, the discharged patient living in the community who is or becomes psychotic and has the freedom to remain so will become a major problem. There is no easy solution, but it is clear that the present one is inadequate. The presence of such patients in the community is neither helpful to the community nor to community acceptance of the mentally ill; most important, it is not helpful to the patient.

Another hazard of treatment is the hazard of diagnoses or of missed diagnoses. We have left, to a large extent, the cloud-cuckoo-land of disinterest in diagnosis or the belief in its nonexistence. This still leaves us, however, with incorrect or imprecise diagnoses, which have led to patients' with affective disorders being treated as schizophrenic and therefore being deprived of an effective treatment as well as being subjected to the side effects of neuroleptic drugs. Sufficient data are now available to show that, given proper training and education, the diagnostic reliability of psychiatrists is quite acceptable. A few years ago seldom a week went by that I did not see a manic-depressive patient misdiagnosed as "schizophrenic." Now I believe it may be said that seldom a month goes by without this happening. Obviously, things are improving but they have quite some way to go.

One thinks of the misdiagnosed organic cases cited by Hunter (1973), of a case of homocystinuria seen by Cuculic, Simpson, and Payne (in preparation), and of a recent case of Wilson's disease by Scheinberg (1975), all of whom were treated inappropriately and who experienced prolonged and unnecessary suffering. A list of such cases could occupy several papers. These hazards result from the movement away from the medical model, and they emphasize the need for adequate diagnostic training in medicine and neurology as well as in psychiatry.

Related to diagnosis is, of course, prognosis, a key problem in treatment. It is well established that schizophrenics, whether they are chronic inpatients or acute, newly discharged outpatients, fare better on maintenance chemotherapy than on a placebo (Hogarty and Goldberg, 1973). However convincing these data may be, the major problem is that we are dealing with statistical significances rather than clinical relevancies. That more people relapse on placebo than on active treatment is an important finding, but the question really is: How should a patient be treated and for how long? Or, coming back to prognosis, which type of patient requires continuous chemotherapy and which type of patient does not? This question has important implications because of the problem of tardive dyskinesia as a side effect of treatment, which I shall discuss later. Attempts to delineate these different prognostic groups have so far been unsuccessful. Ideally, one should, from a historical and psychopathological point of view, be able to diagnose the patients who have acute schizophrenia but are in remission and do not require maintenance medication, perhaps suggesting "nonprocess schizophrenia," "schizophreniform psychosis," "psychogenic psychosis," "reactive psychosis," etc. On an impressionistic basis, such patients are often continued on medication for six to 12 months. Then, somewhat arbitrarily, if they have a second episode, they are continued on medication for twice that period, and if they have a third episode, they are medicated for the rest of their lives. Some clinicians place any patient who has been hospitalized for schizophrenia on continuous, long-term maintenance chemotherapy. This is an unnecessary and hazardous procedure, not only because of the dangers of tardive dyskinesia and other possible drug side effects (skin reactions, eye changes, cardiovascular changes, genitourinary difficulties, etc.) but also from an economic point of view. That it may be unnecessary is even more important from the point of view of the patients' functioning, since a certain sluggishness is apparent in many patients taking chemotherapeutic agents. Indeed, there are studies to show that some patients become worse on medication (Simpson, 1975).

The problem of monitoring blood levels of drugs relates to this latter issue. As of this moment, the amount of medication a patient receives is indeed arbitrary. A patient usually receives medication until his symptoms begin to abate or troublesome side effects appear. Thereafter, he may be maintained on the same dosage indefinitely or the dosage may be dramatically reduced, which often results in an exacerbation of symptoms, or the dosage may be slowly decreased and the patient maintained on what is hoped to be an optimal and therefore minimal dosage of the drug. How to decide on such a dosage is no simple matter. The arbitrary nature of dosage is highlighted when one begins prescribing drugs like clozapine which do not produce extrapyramidal effects where it becomes clear that our major decisions about drug dosages are based on side effects rather than therapeutic efficacy. Indeed, in studies that used changes in handwriting to monitor drug dosages, it appeared that physicians overdosed by 100 percent (Angus and Simpson, 1970). It is now well known that patients receiving the same dose of a neuroleptic may have enormously different blood levels (Cooper and Simpson, 1976). Indeed, we have shown in a group of patients receiving 400 mg of chlorpromazine daily that the levels can range from completely undetectable to very high (e.g., 0 to 230 ng/ml). This is relevant to a study by Curry (1970) who showed that some patients with very high blood levels of drugs are liable to have an exacerbation of their illness. This can occur even with the administration of modest dosages. If it were possible to define a therapeutic window for neuroleptics, as it is with lithium, then a solution to the problem might be found. One would also predict that if the dosage of neuroleptics were regulated according to blood levels, the likelihood of patients' developing tardive dyskinesia would lessen. This condition is frequently claimed to be a dose-related problem; that is, it generally occurs in patients who have been receiving large dosages of neuroleptics over a long period of time. However, since the data about dosages are frequently inaccurate, incomplete, or even contradictory, it might make more sense to look at the plasma levels of drugs since these might correlate more closely with this adverse effect than would dosage prescribed.

To return to the question of who does and who does not need medication: To answer it would require outpatient studies which would have to be placebo-controlled, replicated, and rereplicated, wherein one would try to delineate which patients remain stable while receiving no medication. The number of variables in such studies is likely to be large since a definition of stability is difficult and would obviously depend on such factors as housing, money, community facilities, and the social environment in which the patient lived. A further problem would be the duration of the study, since it is frequently assumed that if one identifies patients who relapse and need medication, this is a permanent situation. Although neuroleptics tend to prevent rehospitalization or psychotic behavior, this is by no means a consistent finding. Despite all of the advances in treatment, many patients capable of living in the community while receiving neuroleptics still develop a schizophrenic defect. One must ask, therefore: When do these patients develop a defect and do they still require neuroleptics? It is possible that these patients reach a plateau at this defect stage without further need for neuroleptic drugs. The latter possibility would indicate cautious withdrawal of medication from all patients who are on continuous maintenance therapy and who appear to be in a stabilized and possibly "defect" state.

There is also the problem of the inability of the "well" patient to believe in the need for treatment and therefore be willing to continue it. Judgment and insight are indeed frequently impaired in schizophrenia. The major value of psychotherapy or group therapy may well rest as much in obtaining the patient's compliance in taking his medication as it does in giving support and help in reality situations. I have seen and known a patient on a research project who received three months of neuroleptics, followed by three months of placebo, followed by three months of neuroleptics. Before he started treatment and during the placebo period, he was a totally disorganized, dishevelled, incontinent, regressed patient who during his period on neuroleptics (or what we correctly assumed were neuroleptics, since it was a double-blind study, was capable of graphing all the study data including his own. At the end of the study, his ups and his downs and what had actually been going on in relation to the active medication were discussed in detail with him. But he could not believe that the medication had anything to do with his being well and, though discharged, he soon returned. Eventually he was capable of maintaining himself in the community; yet the extreme difficulty in getting him to accept a relationship between neuroleptic drugs and his well-being remained.

The introduction of the long-acting drugs has helped to overcome this obstacle to treatment. As they have been used in clinics, where there is a certain amount of group activity, they have had an effect not only on the patients but on the staff, since a patient who fails to come for a long-acting drug injection is more likely to be telephoned or sought after than a patient who merely misses an ordinary clinic visit. Long-acting drugs are of value not only for patients who may refuse medication or be somewhat haphazard in taking it, but, because of their different metabolic pathways, they may be of value to patients who have become "habituated" to their previous oral medication. It is becoming clear that the chronic administration of drugs results in an increase in their metabolism (Kolakowska and Franklin, 1975). In some patients, the possibility exists that a breakdown occurs in the gut or the liver, rendering the drugs practically inactive. Curry, D'Mello, and Mould (1971) demonstrated in isolated guinea-pig ileum loops that only one-sixth of a dose of chlorpromazine is absorbed unchanged. We described a case of enzyme induction in which the patient improved dramatically on a drug and then deteriorated (Cooper et al., 1975). The loss of clinical efficacy associated with a drop to unmeasurable neuroleptic blood levels clearly indicated enzyme induction. The use of a long-acting or parenteral drug of any kind eliminates the possibility of breakdown in the gut as well as the first pass effect through the liver wherein a substantial breakdown of the active drug can occur. Bypassing the gut and the liver with parenteral forms can ensure that the active ingredient gets into the blood stream and ultimately into the central nervous system in adequate quantities. Thus, nonresponders or relapsing patients, whether they are cooperative in taking oral medication or not, are candidates for long-acting drugs.

The fear that long-acting drugs will be more hazardous has not been borne out in clinical practice and one can confidently predict that their use will increase in the long-term treatment of schizophrenia.

Although I have not dealt with the routine side effects or the unwanted effects of neuroleptics, I should like to emphasize some of the hazards of side effects that are apt to be overlooked. The apathy and sluggishness that neuroleptics may produce have been mentioned. They are sometimes related to akinesia and/or weight gain;

the latter can be considerable and is difficult to treat. These effects confound any evaluation of "drive," "apathy," "anergia," "lack of volition," and even socialization and sexuality in medicated patients. Endocrine functions may be disturbed considerably, varying from amenorrhea, breast enlargement or engorgement, false pregnancy tests, and diminished sexual feeling in women, to impotence or disorders of ejaculation in men. Thioridazine is particularly prone to produce the latter, and this should be inquired for. If the patient associates sexual dysfunction with the drug he may stop taking it, whereas it would be wiser to change his prescription to a more potent drug less likely to produce this effect.

Extrapyramidal side effects have been discussed elsewhere (Simpson, 1975). I would merely stress that it is painful to see misdiagnosed or missed dystonic reactions, the failure to recognize or attempt to treat akathisia, or the routine administration of antiparkinson agents which, even if required at some period of treatment, need not be continued even in cases of acute dystonic reactions. Attempts should be made to discontinue such medication (despite an initial indication) after about three months since there is evidence that a large number of patients do not require it after that time (DiMascio, 1971). Antiparkinson agents have their own side effects which are part of the hazards of treatment (Simpson, 1975) and may even contribute to tardive dyskinesia (Kiloh, Smith, and Williams, 1973).

Tardive dyskinesia is another side effect which is receiving considerable attention at the moment. It is usually believed to occur more frequently in women after chronic administration of neuroleptics, particularly if the patients have organic brain disease and have been taking high dosages (Crane, 1973). We should remember, however, that it may occur in men and women in their twenties after only a few months of neuroleptic treatment. A transitory but marked tardive dyskinesia may occur after abrupt discontinuation of high dosages. A patient may become dyskinetic while receiving medication, and one should, therefore, look for early signs of the disease such as facial tics, and tremor or movements of the tongue when it is held within the buccal cavity. The tongue movements frequently are vermicular or fascicular, and they appear long before the mouthing, chewing, pouting, pursing, smacking, and sucking movements frequently associated with frank, rapid, dyskinetic tongue movements, choreoathetoid movements of the hands, arms or feet, akathisia, and other more distinct features of the syndrome. The early signs should prompt a reevaluation of the patient in an attempt to reduce medication which may or may not be successful. Tardive dyskinesia, reversible or irreversible, may be a hazard we will reluctantly accept, if the only other choice is frank psychosis, but we should recognize it.

The social aspect of treatment presents a further hazard, since required facilities in the community often do not exist. This lack mitigates against successful community treatment and is at the same time often associated with community resistance to people who are in any way "different." The widespread discharging of patients into the community has certainly solidified this resistance and produced a negative image of psychiatry and psychiatric patients, together with intense criticism of state hospitals. In many ways it highlights the failure of psychiatry, of the community and, to a large extent, of the community mental health movements to prepare themselves for the changes in psychiatry that were obviously on the way and indeed had taken place in other countries. Thus, the controversy of the psychological therapist versus the somatic therapist which gave way to that of the inpatient doctor versus the outpatient doctor, is now the hospital psychiatrist versus the community psychiatrist. Here again the legal position that results in keeping people out of the hospital is pitted against community pressures to hospitalize patients who are chronically ill, difficult, bad, or who have just nowhere else to go. At the same time, middle-class judgments are made as to what is or is not best for essentially working-class patients. Thus, well-meaning people want lovely places in the community for patients who deserve them but who, in fact, are often indifferent to their environment. In the absence of such idealized situations, the patient may well remain hospitalized waiting for such places to open. An educational program is certainly required to raise understanding of schizophrenia, what it means and what it does to people. We should know that schizophrenic patients sometimes survive better in a single room than in any other type of situation (Brown, 1959). This may be painful for people to accept; it is a certain admission of failure of treatment, but it is a fact. Similarly, it is important that all people involved in their care and treatment realize that schizophrenic patients do develop defects. Their lack of volition, blunting of affect, and apathy described so well a hundred years ago are now often viewed as drug-induced apathy, resulting in pressure to withdraw medication which may well be essential to the patients' well-being. A patient in an outpatient clinic lacking a unified team philosophy of treatment may become sandwiched between two different treaters, both believing themselves correct. As always, the patient will suffer.

The referral of patients for treatment in the early stages of an illness is greatly influenced by the current treatment philosophy. Frequently, the notion that one or another type of psychotherapy is vitally important is voiced. Thus, an evaluation of treatments, as presented in the foregoing chapter by Philip R. A. May, might convey that much of this problem is solved. Regrettably, for a large number of people in the country, May might as well never have carried out his elegant studies, written his book, and continued to write and talk on the subject, because it falls on deaf ears. One cannot assume that research, carefully executed, can affect treatment when the research results run against the current treatment ideology.

Pharmacotherapy is still seen as a treatment of second choice given second-class citizens, often by second-class psychiatrists. This view is beginning to change, but a vast educational program is required in universities and elsewhere to place psychopharmacology in the position it deserves, particularly in the treatment and rehabilitation of schizophrenic patients.

Nevertheless, we should not fall into the trap of overstating the case for psychopharmacology. The data to date suggest that, despite what has been done since chlorpromazine was introduced, the actual impact on the life history of the illness of the majority of schizophrenic patients has changed only slightly since the days of Bleuler. However, new drugs, better training in psychopharmacology, the growth of outpatient and community clinics, and halfway houses may raise the possibility of a somewhat rosier future.

Finally, the current climate surrounding research involving human beings, and mental health research in particular, probably represents the greatest hazard to adequate treatment in the immediate and distant future.

REFERENCES

ANGUS, J. W. S. and SIMPSON, G. M. 1970. Handwriting changes and response to drugs. A controlled study. *Acta Psychiat. Scand. (Suppl.)*, 212:28-37.

BROWN, G. W. 1959. Experiences of discharged chronic schizophrenic patients in various types of living group. *Milbank Memorial Fund Quarterly*, 37 (2):105-131.

COOPER, T. B., SIMPSON, G. M., HAHER, E. J., and BERGNER, P.-E. E. 1975. Butaperazine pharmacokinetics. *Arch. Gen. Psychiatry*, 32:903-905.

COOPER, T. B. and SIMPSON, G. M. 1976. Plasma-blood level monitoring techniques in psychiatry. In L. Gottschalk and S. Merlis (eds.), *Pharmacokinetics of Psychoactive Drugs*. New York: Spectrum Press.

CRANE, G. E. 1973. Persistent dyskinesia. *Br. J. Psychiatry*, 122:395-405.

CURRY, S. H. 1970. Theoretical changes in drug distribution resulting from changes in binding to plasma proteins and to tissues. *J. Pharm. Pharmacol.*, 22:753-757.

CURRY, S. H., D'MELLO, A., and MOULD, G. M. 1971. Destruction of chlorpromazine during absorption in the rat in vivo and in vitro. *Br. J. Pharmacol.*, 42:403-411.

DIMASCIO, A. 1971. Toward a more rational use of antiparkinson drugs in psychiatry. *Drug Therapy*, 1:23-29.

HOGARTY, G. E. and GOLDBERG, S. L. 1973. Collaborative study group. Drug and sociotherapy in the aftercare of schizophrenic patients: One year relapse rates. *Arch. Gen. Psychiatry*, 28:54-64.

HUNTER, R. 1973. Psychiatry and neurology. *Proc. R. Soc. Med.*, 66:359-364.

KILOH, L. G., SMITH, J. S., and WILLIAMS, S. E. 1973. Antiparkinson drugs in psychiatry. *Drug Therapy*, 1:23-29.

KOLAKOWSKA, T. and FRANKLIN, M. 1975. Effect of long-term phenothiazine treatment on drug metabolism. *British Journal of Clinical Pharmacology*, 2:25-28.

SCHEINBERG, H. 1975. A psychogenetic anecdote. *Psychosom. Med.*, 34 (4):368-371.

SIMPSON, G. M. 1975. CNS effects of neuroleptic agents. *Psychiatric Annals*, 5 (11): 53-60.

4

Strategies for Chronic Psychotics

EDWIN E. JOHNSTONE, M.D.
THOMM K. ROBERTS, PH.D. and
JAMES L. CLAGHORN, M.D.

> *It's a poor sort of memory,*
> *the Queen remarked, "that*
> *only works backwards."*
>
> —Lewis Carroll
> *Through the Looking Glass*

Revolutionary changes in mental hospitals lead to mistaken impressions. Abolishing the back wards is not the same as abolishing the problems of the patients who resided there. Shorter hospital stays and declining bed census should not obscure the fact that being out of the hospital is not necessarily the same as being better (Erickson, 1975). Outpatient clinics are being populated by incompletely treated psychotic patients, their problems "swept under the rug" as the patients are swept into the community. One could say that the mental hospital back wards have not been abolished but have been transported into the community, where we have created a new counterpart of the old back ward. The outpatient clinic may indeed be the custodial institution of the 1970s.

The National Institute of Mental Health's biometry division has documented the decline in mental hospital bed census. The census was falling at a rate of 3 percent per year in 1955, accelerating recently to 14 percent per year (Gunderson et al., 1974). California managed to reduce its state hospital population by 70 percent in less than seven years. But in California and New York public protest has

53

arisen over the rush to empty the hospitals without providing out-patient clinics to meet the considerable needs of this multitude of severely ill patients.

When the patient reaches the custodial outpatient clinics he is expected to stabilize, but he is usually not expected to reach better levels of functioning with continuing treatment. Generally assessed in maintenance terms, against maintenance goals, clinic programs aim for stable patterns of attendance, stable ingestion of medication, low dropout rate, low rehospitalization rate. Treatment goals are usually so modest that a patient is considered well managed if he regains his premorbid, even though marginal, level of functioning.

Stabilization is far from utopia. The typical stabilized chronic psychotic patient is indeed marginal. More than a third of patients who were steadily employed before onset of psychosis will become permanently unemployed. Patients who experienced some employment problems before becoming psychotic stand a very poor chance of being successfully employed. Chronic psychotic patients have been able to achieve harmony in tolerant, sheltered, living-working settings (called lodges) which accommodate to the patients' limitations rather than correct them. But when these patients leave the lodge and attempt to become assimilated in the community, they usually fail. Only a scant few clinic patients approach the average level of functioning of their communities (Erickson, 1975).

If the clinics are today's counterparts of the old mental hospital back wards, we need a modern outpatient counterpart of the old "Total Push" program. This could be the "expanded milieu" program for which Philip R. A. May pleads in Chapter 2. Plainly, the needs of these patients are staggering, but research reports indicate that therapeutic nihilism is unjustified and that these patients can accomplish more than has been expected of them.

RESEARCH FINDINGS

Despite the plethora of research reports on hospital treatment of chronic schizophrenic patients, there are few careful studies on outpatient treatment. Most outpatient therapy studies assess effectiveness in terms of maintenance functions. Only a small number address the possibilities of actual improvement in the patients' functional status or severity of symptoms.

Anthony (1972) suggests that the mere availability of outpatient treatment, whatever its emphasis, leads to a reduction of recidivism. He asserts that a patient independent enough to accept separation from the hospital, moderately supported by a group in the community or engaged in minimum counselor contact, has the best prognosis for community adjustment.

Donlon (1973) describes a program in which chronic schizophrenic outpatients were offered refreshments and an informal social experience. They responded with better attendance and began to seek rather than avoid socialization. Donlon cites the modest cost and effort of this approach compared to less effective, costlier, traditional ones. Masnick et al. (1971) report similar good results from a clinic in which patients gathered for informal discussions before seeing their doctors and receiving medication. It is notable that custodial clinic care can be effectively implemented at modest cost and with low, intensity of staff-patient contact.

One of the studies documenting patient change in outpatient psychotherapy came from our clinic (Claghorn et al., 1974). We found that chronic schizophrenic patients receiving a combination of group psychotherapy and neuroleptic drugs showed significant shifts in perception of self and others. One consequence of the combined drug-group psychotherapy approach was that patients began to see themselves more realistically. There were indications that the patients had become more aware of their limitations and had come to grips with the realities of their difficulties in relation to others. Group therapy sessions were low-pressure, concentrating on the tasks of daily existence. As May has observed, such group therapy is more effective when it centers on practical problem-solving and on cooperation with drug treatment rather than on insight and depth of psychological comprehension.

A recent study in our day treatment center attempted to characterize the stabilized chronic schizophrenic patients who are candidates for that program. The study also examined the patients' perceptions of what they find therapeutic in the program. In the first part of the study, a modified version of the Leary Interpersonal Battery was used, along with Meltzoff's Outpatient Adjustment Rating Scales adapted for self-rating. Patients showed a strong tendency to deny pathology, perceiving themselves as interpersonally and socially better adjusted than they were in the eyes of the clinicians. The patients did tend, however, to see significant others in a somewhat glorified way: extremely socially acceptable and dominant. Despite a tendency to gloss over their deficits, the patients acknowledged a discrepancy between their adjustment and that of others (see Figure 1 and Table 1).

In the second part of the study, patients discharged from the day treatment center were asked to complete a questionnaire giving their

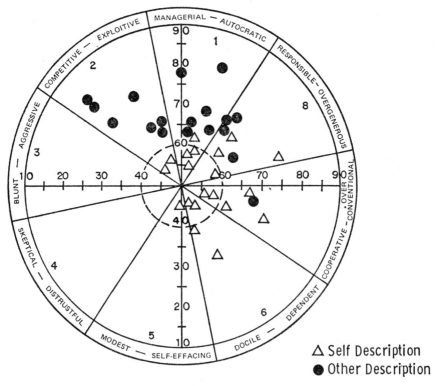

△ Self Description
● Other Description

FIGURE 1

Description of self and description of others (scores of 20 day treatment center patients on a modified version of the Leary Interpersonal Battery).

TABLE 1

SELF DESCRIPTION

Socially Acceptable Behavior
vs.
Socially Undesirable Behavior

Acceptable (Octants 1, 2, 7, 8)	Undesirable (Octants 3, 4, 5, 6)	X²	Sign Level
15	5	5.00	p .05

Affiliation vs. Opposition

Affiliation (Octants 1, 6, 7, 8)	Opposition (Octants 2, 3, 4, 5)	X²	Sign Level
17	3	9.80	p .01

OTHER DESCRIPTION

Socially Acceptable Behavior
vs.
Socially Undesirable Behavior

Acceptable (Octants 1, 2, 7, 8)	Undesirable (Octants 3, 4, 5, 6)	X²	Sign Level
18	0	18.00	p .001

Dominance vs. Submission

Dominance (Octants 1, 2, 3, 8)	Submission (Octants 4, 5, 6, 7)	X²	Sign Level
17	1	14.22	p .001

Table 2

Were Any of the Following Aspects of the Day Hospital Program
Helpful? (42 patients completed this section)

Therapy	Always # (%)	Generally # (%)	Sometimes # (%)	Seldom # (%)	No Response # (%)
Specific advice	16 (38)	14 (33)	11 (26)	1 (2)	0 (0)
Group discussion	19 (45)	9 (32)	12 (29)	1 (2)	1 (2)
Individual counseling	21 (50)	7 (17)	7 (17)	4 (10)	3 (7)
Medication	19 (45)	10 (24)	5 (12)	8 (19)	0 (0)
Transactional analysis	17 (40)	7 (17)	6 (14)	10 (24)	2 (5)
Vocational					
Practice in job interviewing	8 (19)	4 (10)	5 (12)	15 (36)	10 (24)
Contact with vocational rehabilitation program	7 (17)	6 (14)	5 (12)	14 (33)	10 (24)
Avocational					
Recreational therapy	17 (40)	11 (26)	6 (14)	5 (12)	3 (7)
Occupational therapy	12 (29)	12 (29)	6 (14)	10 (24)	2 (5)
Drama	7 (17)	7 (17)	11 (26)	13 (31)	4 (10)
Other	1 (2)	0 (0)	0 (0)	1 (2)	40 (95)

impression of the treatment. We sent out 101 questionnaires; 29 were returned by the patients; 16 were completed by telephoning patients who failed to return the questionnaire. Altogether we have information from 45 of 101 patients. Information of this sort is, of course, fraught with uncertainties, but it deserves inspection. Ninety-six percent of the respondents stated that the day treatment center program had helped them. At least 60 percent indicated that they had been discharged because of the progress they had made.

Eighty-seven percent were living with family members; 9 percent lived alone; only 4 percent lived in some other arrangement. Eighty-four percent stated that they were in good physical condition; over half that number were either employed or engaged in school or vocational training. They tended to attribute the benefits they had received to increased self-understanding and self-reliance (see Table 2).

In looking at the patients' impressions of program elements some patterns emerge. Patients showed more belief in conventional staff contacts than in less conventional approaches. They tended to value specific advice from the therapists; this might well have been a major appeal of the individual counseling and group discussions. These patients did not put much stock in transactional analysis and drama, although these approaches are said to be suited to patients' communication needs. The usual "arts and crafts" kind of occupational therapy was similarly discounted by the patients; they credited recreational therapy more than the latter three approaches. Medication was ranked as one of the effective therapies, which indicates that patients could see tangible benefits from the drugs comparable to those of counseling.

When these patients were treated in the day center, vocational counseling was part of the program, but vocation-related activities were not pursued in any systematic manner. The patients seemed to indicate that they found those experiences irrelevant and of questionable value. Such findings should result in a revamping of the services offered to meet the unique needs of patients with occupational problems.

Although these patients deny their own pathology, they are able, nevertheless, to make critical discriminations. Their preferences are distinct, and they reflect critical judgment which should be taken into account.

These findings agree with those of our earlier study (Claghorn et al., 1974) in which we suggested that chronic schizophrenic outpatients can profit from group psychotherapy that is nonthreatening, but direct and deficit-confronting. With such an approach the patients begin to identify their problems more accurately and to disclose them. Then the acknowledged problems become amenable to direct advice and problem-solving discussion.

The role of neuroleptic drugs can hardly be overemphasized (although some writers have managed to do this). May and Tuma (1964) declare that, in hospital settings, drugs alone account for the major part of patient improvement. These authors found little contribution by behavioral therapies and psychotherapy. Perhaps this is true in hospital settings, but it is not so in the clinic. In an outpatient clinic, Hogarty et al. (1974) demonstrated additive effects of chlorpromazine and advice-providing counseling, which they dubbed "major role therapy."

Symptoms that Bleuler viewed as fundamental to schizophrenia are profoundly affected by neuroleptic drugs. Secondary symptoms respond even more strikingly. Hollister (1972) has found that severely dysphoric, highly agitated patients respond best to higher doses of neuroleptics, while patients with hallucinations and prominent thought disorders respond best to lower doses. Social factors and illness patterns are also determinants. Klerman (1970) found that private patients with good pre-hospital social adjustment and favorable history of illness are more likely to respond well to drugs (and to placebos) than are chronically ill, often-admitted patients with poor social adjustment who frequent public institutions.

Drugs alone, despite their nearly miraculous effects, are limited in what they can accomplish. They sometimes are not sufficient to eradicate such actively elaborated symptoms as hallucinations, delusions, and bizarre behavior. Chemotherapy by itself cannot do much to counter deficit symptoms like social ineptness, fragility of logical thought processes, social withdrawal, or feebleness of self-assertion. The limitations of chemotherapy illustrate the need to augment drug treatment with psychotherapy and behavior-based treatment.

Patients whose persistent hallucinations were not abolished by drugs have been shown in the hospital to respond to reinforcement and punishment (Anderson and Alpert, 1974) or to relaxation training and systematic desensitization (Slade, 1972). Paradoxical intention has often been shown to eradicate drug-resistant hallucinations and obsessive thought processes. Patients showing bizarre behavior may respond to behavior-contingent time-outs (Cayner and Kiland, 1974) or to paradoxical prescriptions.

Operant conditioning approaches in the hospital have been useful for treating deficit symptoms. Idle hospital patients may be induced by reinforcement to increase working behavior, even by using sitting as the reinforcer (Mitchell and Stoffelmayr, 1973). Mute patients may have speech restored through use of a variety of reinforcers (Cliffe, 1974; Thompson, Fraser, and McDougall, 1974).

Therapeutic approaches that employ cognitive processes are especially useful in treating deficit symptoms of schizophrenic outpatients. Socially withdrawn and socially inept patients have responded to assertive training. Such training in an outpatient group diminished the patients' social anxieties while it increased their interpersonal skills (Bloomfield, 1973). Schizophrenic patients can be trained to improve their performance on tasks that require sustained attention, thought, or language skills (Meichenbaum and Cameron, 1973). Taught to logically talk themselves (first overtly, then covertly) through tasks, these patients developed concentration and attention. Schizophrenics can be trained similarly to acquire defined social skills (Goldsmith and McFall, 1975). Cognition-based behavior therapies, developed mainly in other settings, may have more promise for persons in outpatient social rehabilitation programs.

DISCUSSION

In considering management of chronic schizophrenic patients outside the hospital, several crucial issues deserve more elaboration.

Goals

It is a serious error to set only custodial goals for outpatient care without realizing that more ambitious therapeutic goals are appropriate and attainable. Clinics should begin to assess their functioning not only in custodial terms, but in terms of relevant changes in the patients. The Texas Research Institute recently changed the name of its medication maintenance clinic to social rehabilitation clinic. Name changes, of course, are not enough, but they do promote clarity of thought in relation to goals.

Generalization and Permanence

Patients may show encouraging changes in a treatment setting without the appearance of similar changes in their living or working situation. To equate a patient's good functioning in the clinic with improved experience in the real world could be a serious error.

Techniques to extend improved performance into the patients' home lives have eluded us so far. Patients who demonstrate higher functional levels after intensive treatment show a decay in their condition when their clinic contacts are spaced farther apart. Within two years most patients lose the gains they have made as a result of intensive treatment. Perhaps deleterious family influences gradually take their toll, or the simple absence of proper reinforcers allows gradual extinction of acquired desirable behavior patterns. Techniques that generate lasting changes are needed.

Relevant Psychotherapy Research

Many researchers of psychotherapy with schizophrenic patients display an elitist orientation, focusing on psychoanalytically based therapy with patients who have an unusually favorable prognosis. Such research is hardly relevant to the real needs of public psychiatric clinics. We need to know what works for the majority of patients within the realistic limits of program resources. We may, at least, be nearing the point where extremists no longer insist that psychotherapy exclude concomitant chemotherapy (Friedman, Gunderson, and Feinsilver, 1973).

Other Issues

One provocative research question is: How intense should therapy be? High intensity and formality could prove to be countertherapeutic. In our study (Claghorn et al., 1974), we were surprised that patients with rather spotty attendance at weekly group meetings showed significant shifts at the end of treatment. One might suspect that these patients selected the degree of intensity that suited them best. Perhaps one level of intensity is optimum for custodial goals, another for therapeutic goals.

Ludwig (1968) describes a method of engaging chronic patients in therapy through a complexly orchestrated inpatient treatment program that takes advantage of diverse approaches, but he reports regretfully that only one of three patients became involved and responded. Similar obstacles block the effort to provide more effective outpatient treatment. Homogeneously applied "milieu" or "token economy" approaches may disregard individual needs and may fail to reach some patients who require a unique approach. Allen and Magaro (1971) stress the need to identify and group patients according to their individual requirements. Until we have reliable predictors we shall have to rely on accurate early identification of specific measures that are effective for a specific patient.

The Ideal Clinic

Bearing in mind the matters discussed, what would be the ideal clinic for chronic schizophrenic patients? A hospitable, nonthreatening, fairly informal setting would draw the patients into forming a favorable rapport and insure reliable attendance. Prepared to be responsible for the patient for an indefinite span of years, such a clinic would maintain aggressive re-contact with patients who attempt to drop out of treatment. The staff would strive for the best possible attitude of patients toward medication. Drug prescriptions would not be thoughtlessly refilled. Instead, the optimum dosage and drug effects would be sought at all times, adjusted to the patient's changing needs.

Others in the patient's life setting would be engaged energetically in the patient's treatment. Their rapport, too, would be sought. They would be guided in establishing behavior reinforcers to sustain the patient in ideal function. If the patient's own family were to be uncooperative with the therapeutic enterprise, alternative living arrangements would be made available. The patient and his living mates might receive periodic "booster shots" of retraining in behavior modification. Similar involvement with employers and prospective employers would assure that experiences on the job also involved reinforcement of desired behavior. Rehabilitation counselors would be integral to the clinic, not only to provide special training experiences in the clinic, but also to act as a bridge, perhaps on occasion accompanying the patient to the job.

Whatever deficiencies they may have in common, patients do not have the same needs. A problem-oriented approach to management assures the patient of unique treatment that addresses his needs and involves him in activities tailor-made to his particular strengths and deficits. As Erickson (1975) observed, "What to teach to whom in the way of problem-solving skills and how to teach them is a virtually unexplored clinical and research area." It may be useful to deal deliberately with the issue of self-perception. One simple device is to have the patient and the staff prepare separate weekly report cards that grade the patient's relevant problem areas. The discrepancy between staff- and self-grading highlights the patient's need for more accurate self-assessment.

Since what counts is the patient's experience in the real world, not in the clinic, we need social rehabilitation measures that assess the patient's functioning in the most objective manner possible. Standardization of social rehabilitation measures would set the stage for program evaluation and program comparison. Programs would no longer be measured in administrative terms (discharge, length of stay) which can be manipulated and are only indirectly related to patient condition, but in terms of lasting gains from treatment.

Conclusion

If we could have a memory that worked forward as well as backward, we might see that what we thought we knew about schizophrenia is no longer true. The picture we had of schizophrenic patients was determined largely by the uniformity, consistency, and security of hospital environments which helped to render these patients unresponsive to psychotherapy. The diversity and demands of community living may influence social functioning and illness patterns that are less predictable than those of the past. It is an undisputed fact that the pattern of prominent presenting symptoms has changed radically (Gunderson et al., 1974), so that hebephrenic and catatonic syndromes are vanishing rapidly from the scene. With further social changes and more psychotherapeutic research we might find that the majority of chronic schizophrenic patients will respond to specially adapted psychotherapies.

REFERENCES

Allen, D. J. and Magaro, P. A. 1971. Measures of change in token economy programs. *Behav. Res. Ther.*, 9:311-318.

ANDERSON, L. T. and ALPERT, M. J. 1974. Operant analysis of hallucination frequency in a hospitalized schizophrenic. *Journal of Behavior Therapy and Experimental Psychiatry*, 51:13-18.

ANTHONY, W. A., BUELL, G. J., SHARRAT, S., and ALTHOFF, M. 1972. Efficacy of psychiatric rehabilitation. *Psychol. Bull.*, 78:447-456.

BLOOMFIELD, H. H. 1973. Assertive training in an outpatient group of chronic schizophrenics: A preliminary report. *Behavior Therapy*, 4: 277-281.

CAYNER, J. J. and KILAND, J. R. 1974. Use of brief time-out with three schizophrenic patients. *Journal of Behavior Therapy and Experimental Psychiatry*, 5:141-145.

CLAGHORN, J. L., JOHNSTONE, E. E., COOK, T. H., and ITSCHNER, L. 1974. Group therapy and maintenance treatment of schizophrenics. *Arch. Gen. Psychiatry*, 31:361-365.

CLIFFE, M. J. 1974. Reinstatement of speech in mute schizophrenics by operant conditioning. *Acta Psychiatr. Scand.*, 6:577-585.

DONLON, P. T., RADA, R. T., and KNIGHT, S. W. 1973. A therapeutic aftercare setting for "refractory" chronic schizophrenic patients. *Am. J. Psychiatry*, 130:682-684.

ERICKSON, R. C. 1975. Outcome studies in mental hospitals: A review. *Psychol. Bull.*, 82:519-540.

FRIEDMAN, R. J., GUNDERSON, J. G., and FEINSILVER, D. B. 1973. The psychotherapy of schizophrenia: An NIMH program. *Am. J. Psychiatry*, 130:674-677.

GOLDSMITH, J. B. and McFALL, R. M. 1975. Development and evaluation of an interpersonal skill-training program for psychiatric inpatients. *J. Abnorm. Psychol.*, 84:51-58.

GUNDERSON, J. G., AUTRY, J. H., MOSHER, L. R., and BUCHSBAUM, S. 1974. Special report: Schizophrenia 1973. *Schizophrenia Bulletin*, 9:16-54.

HOGARTY, G. E., GOLDBERG, S. C., SCHOOLER, N. R., ULRICH, R. F. and The Collaborative Study Group. 1974. Drug and sociotherapy in the aftercare of schizophrenic patients: Two-year relapse rates. *Arch. Gen. Psychiatry*, 31:603-608.

HOLLISTER, L. E. 1972. Optimum use of antipsychotic drugs. *Curr. Psychiatr. Ther.*, 12:81-88.

KLERMAN, G. L., GOLDBERG, S. G., and DAVIS, D. 1970. Relationship between the hospital milieu and the response to phenothiazines in the treatment of schizophrenics. *Acta Psychiatr. Belg.* 70:716-729.

LUDWIG, A. M. 1968. The influence of nonspecific healing techniques with chronic schizophrenics. *Am. J. Psychiatry*, 22:382-404.

MASNICK, R., BUCCI, L., ISENBERG, D., and NORMAND, W. 1961. "Coffee and . . .": A way to treat the untreatable. *Am. J. Psychiatry*, 128: 56-59.

MAY, P. R. A. and TUMA, A. H. 1964. The effect of psychotherapy and Stelazine on length of hospital stay, release rate and supplemental treatment of schizophrenic patients. *J. Nerv. Ment. Dis.* 139:362-369.

MEICHENBAUM, D. and CAMERON, R. 1973. Training schizophrenics to talk to themselves: A means of developing attentional controls. *Behavior Therapy*, 4:515-534.

MITCHELL, W. S. and STOFFELMAYR, B. E. 1973. Application of the Premack principle to the behavioral control of extremely inactive schizophrenics. *J. Appl. Behav. Anal.*, 6:419-423.

SLADE, P. D. 1972. The effects of systematic desensitization on auditory hallucinations. *Behav. Res. Ther.* 10:85-91.

THOMPSON, N., FRASER, D., and McDOUGALL, A. 1974. The reinstatement of speech in near-mute chronic schizophrenics by instruction, imitative prompts and reinforcement. *Journal of Behavior Therapy and Experimental Psychiatry*, 1:83-89.

Part II

RESEARCH IN TREATMENT TECHNIQUES IN PSYCHONEUROSIS

5

Psychoneurosis: Integrating Pharmacotherapy and Psychotherapy

GERALD L. KLERMAN, M.D.

In the treatment of psychoneuroses, pharmacotherapy is frequently combined with psychotherapy of various forms: individual, group, family, or behavior modification. Despite the widespread use of these therapeutic combinations, their scientific bases are limited. To attain a firm understanding of combined drug-psychotherapy for psychoneuroses, scientific knowledge is ideally necessary in four areas: evidence for the efficacy of each of the treatments, alone and in combination; understanding of their respective modes of action; knowledge of their interactions, positive and negative; and psychophysiological and psychopathological concepts that bridge the pharmacological and psychotherapeutic approaches. The attainment of such knowledge is not likely for a number of years because serious obstacles exist in the conduct of therapeutic research, including theoretical and conceptual complexities, methodological difficulties, and intraprofessional conflicts.

I shall attempt to clarify some of the theoretical and conceptual complexities inherent in combining treatments. Insufficient attention has been given to the integration of these therapeutic approaches. A number of questions need to be asked: What effects does the introduction of drug therapy have on the psychotherapeutic process and outcome? Conversely, what effects does the addition of psychotherapy have on drug treatment? What are the interactions—positive and negative—between drugs and psychotherapy? Under what conditions do drugs facilitate or retard psychotherapeutic communication? Will rapid reduction of symptoms remove the patient's motivation for insight? These and similar questions require careful theoretical analysis in order for controlled research to be designed and executed.

Focus on Depression

Because the scope of clinical states subsumed under the term "psychoneuroses" is so vast, I shall focus on the depressive neuroses. I do this for a number of reasons. First, this is an area in which I have worked extensively. Second, impressive research has been done on the efficacy of psychotherapy and pharmacotherapy for depression. Third, the approach developed in this paper can be extended to the treatment of such psychoneurotic conditions as phobia, conversion, compulsions, and dissociative states.

Scientific Knowledge and Professional Ideology

The Clinician's Dilemma:
What To Do When There Is a Paucity of Evidence

As stated above, an ideal assessment of the theoretical and therapeutic aspects of combined psychotherapy and drug therapy requires empirical evidence about the efficacy and safety of each therapy. With respect to the efficacy and safety of antidepressant drug therapy, the quantity and quality of the evidence is favorable. Since the mid-1950s many controlled clinical trials have demonstrated the efficacy of the tricyclic antidepressants, the monoamine oxidase inhibitors, phenothiazines, and lithium compared to placebo or other control. For symptom relief and resolution of the acute depressive episode, drug therapy has demonstrated efficacy. Moreover, there is now substantial evidence for the value of two classes of drugs for maintenance therapy to prevent relapse and recurrence: lithium for both bipolar and unipolar depressions and the tricyclics for unipolar recurrent depressions and neurotic depressions characterized by relapse and fluctuation (Klerman et al., 1974).

Evidence for the efficacy of psychotherapy for depression is more limited but improving rapidly. Even though the efficacy of psychotherapy is itself a subject of continual controversy, there are now six controlled studies showing the efficacy of psychotherapy for depression (Luborsky, Singer, and Luborsky, 1975). Studies have reported individual psychotherapy done by social workers (Weissman et al., 1974), family therapy (Friedman, 1975), and group therapy (Covi et al., 1974). These three studies report therapies that attempt to modify the patient's interpersonal patterns. Some newer psychotherapies are based on social behaviorism, particularly derived from the research of Lewinsohn in Oregon (1974). Peter McLean (1975), one of Lewinsohn's students, reported results of a controlled trial that demonstrated efficacy of behavioral therapy. At the 1975 meeting of the Society for Psychotherapy Research, Beck and Rush reported a pilot study on the efficacy of cognitive behavioral therapy that showed it to be equivalent to tricyclic antidepressant therapy (Rush, 1975). At the same meeting, Shaw reported results of group treatment based on both cognitive and behavioral theories of depression (Shaw, 1975).

Evidence in support of combined treatment has emerged slowly. In a comprehensive review of controlled studies of the efficacy of psychotherapy, Luborsky identified nine published studies on the combination of drugs and psychotherapy. Eight of the studies showed efficacy for the combination over and above the individual constituents alone (Luborsky, Singer, and Luborsky, 1975).

Drugs and psychotherapy derive from different theoretical realms and a priori should be neutral to each other, but ideologically they are competitive. Although considerable psychophysiological research has been done in animals and man to document the possible mechanisms by which conflict and stress influence endocrine activity, amine metabolism, and brain function (particularly via pituitary, hypothalamic, and subcortical mechanisms), experimentally based formulations are rare for the use of psychotherapy combined with drug therapy. Recent psychobiological studies in psychophysiology, biofeedback, and neurochemistry provide more sophisticated insights into bio-behavioral interaction. These insights may break the theoretical mind-body dualism so tenaciously held by adherents of biological and psychotherapeutic approaches in psychology and psychiatry.

Drug therapy produces significant changes, not only in target symptoms, but also in psychodynamic functioning. Theoretically, studies of the actions of antidepressant drugs involve the possible relationship of central nervous system (CNS) substrates to affect, ego functions, and symptom formation. Ostow (1967) interpreted drug effects in terms of psychoanalytic libidinal theory. Sarwer-Foner (1960), Azima (1961), Bellak and Rosenberg (1966), and other psychoanalysts emphasized drug effects on ego functions. Changes in sleep mechanisms and patterns as a result of drugs have also undergone psychodynamic study. Kramer, Whitman, and colleagues (1968) placed emphasis on drug-induced changes in dream content. In addition, there have been studies of drug effects on hostility, anxiety, and other affects (Gottschalk et al., 1965; Klerman and Gershon, 1970). Further studies in this area offer promise of elucidating psychodynamic mechanisms involved in antidepressant drug actions; conversely, experimental alterations of CNS amines by pharmacological means could clarify the role of neurochemical substrates in the psychodynamics of affect regulation.

As promising as these developments are, they do not provide the quantity and quality of evidence that justify clinical decisions concerning the choice of treatment.

The Role of Professional Ideologies

Faced with this situation, the practicing psychiatrist empirically prescribes combinations of drugs and psychotherapy for the treatment of depression. In so doing, clinicians often act in conflict with their stated theoretical persuasions and therapeutic preferences. Almost all studies of the attitudes and values of American psychiatrists have found that the physicians give greatest primacy and value to individual psychotherapy, and that they hold drug therapy in low esteem while acknowledging its efficacy for symptom reduction.

Since the introduction of drug therapy in the mid-1950s, American psychiatrists and clinical psychologists have been divided in their attitudes toward the value of drugs in the treatment of psychoneuroses, whether alone or in combination with psychotherapy. It is possible to identity four groups of clinicians: the proponents of drug therapy, the skeptics, the radical critics, and the pragmatic combiners. I shall review the points of view expressed by members of these four groups and critically analyze the conceptual and theoretical models proposed.

The Proponents of Drug Therapy

Many psychiatrists argue in favor of a causal relationship between the introduction of modern drug therapy and the improvements that occurred during the treatment of the mentally ill, including depressed patients—particularly those hospitalized with psychotic depressions—but also the ambulatory psychoneurotic patients. This view has been most widely held by mental health professionals working in public mental health institutions with severely ill patients, but it is also advanced by a large number of practitioners in private settings and outpatient clinics who belong to what Hollingshead and Redlich (1958) identified as the "directive and organic" group of practitioners. These psychiatrists, along with many journalists and public officials, concluded that the new drugs not only improved patient treatment but brought about a revolution in psychiatry, putting psychiatry back into the "mainstream" of modern medicine. Many proponents of drug therapy have an implicit, at times exquisite, antitherapeutic and antipsychotherapeutic bias and regard the success of drug therapy as support for their long-held criticism of Freudianism and related psychotherapeutic theories.

The proponents of pharmacotherapy of depression include many former advocates of electroconvulsive therapy (ECT) and such strong adherents of lithium as Nathan Kline (1974) and Ronald Fieve (1975), who often combined their support of ECT and drug therapy with criticism of psychotherapy as valueless or at best of unproven efficacy.

The Skeptics

The skeptics comprise private practitioners skilled in psychotherapy, many clinical psychologists, and a large group of social psychologists and researchers who questioned whether the new tranquilizers and related drugs had any "real" effect. Psychiatry witnessed periods of enthusiasm and optimism for such new treatments as mesmerism in the 18th century, moral treatment and phrenology in the 19th century, and numerous other fads for both psychic and somatic treatments. The skeptics pointed to the extensive research in industrial settings on the Hawthorne effect whereby any increase in attention and enthusiasm had a positive effect on a group situation, ameliorating conflict and increasing the productivity of workers. The skeptics wondered if similar enthusiasm and attention on the part of previously pessimistic and nihilistic physicians could be communicated to patients and their families. This Hawthorne effect of clinician's zeal would then interact positively with the placebo effect of the patient's participation and expectations. Perhaps the therapeutic benefits attributed to drugs were the result of social-psychological forces rather than the pharmacologic actions of the drugs on the central nervous system.

The Radical Critics

While the skeptics raised questions, the radical critics were openly derogatory of these drugs. Not only were the drugs little more than placebo, but more importantly they were actually detrimental to the patient's welfare and had adverse effects on the patient, the psychiatrist, and the family. Drug therapy impaired the patient's progress in psychotherapy by increasing reliance on biological treatment, fostering dependency on the physician, and blunting capacity for insight. In addition to these deleterious effects, the new tranquilizing drugs were regarded as having even more harmful effects on psychotherapists, limiting their skill by their latent tendencies to find quick solutions to complex social problems. Similar concerns were expressed about the family who would see drug treatment as an explanation of the patient's illness in terms of "nerves" and "real illness" rather than face the conflict, guilt, and other psychological issues that may involve personal responsibility and the need for change in life-style or family practices. The radical critics challenged the medical model as authoritarian and biological and stated that in prescribing drugs physicians used chemical straight jackets or participated in the maintenance of conformity in this repressive society.

Implicit in this viewpoint is the concept of "negative placebo effect." Feminist therapists come closest to expressing this point of view concerning the treatment of depression. They propose that pharmacotherapy hinders "true feminist" psychotherapy because it regards the depressed woman's problems as biomedical and deflects the patient's attention from consciousness-raising efforts and ultimately from social change that would end sexism and promote equality.

The Pragmatic Combiners

The largest group of practitioners have been eclectic and pragmatic. Whatever their theoretical orientation, in practice they have prescribed drugs with increasing frequency. They often combine drugs with psychotherapy on a trial-and-error basis, but the theoretical justifications for this practice remain vague.

By prescribing drugs in combination with the psychotherapy of depression, psychiatrists expect the drugs to reduce manifest symptoms and lower the subjective distress of the patient. Such prominent symptoms as anxiety, insomnia, tension, and autonomic nervous system irregularities become the targets for drug prescription. The psychiatrist hopes thereby to facilitate communication, to reduce resistance to therapeutic insight, and to accelerate psychotherapeutic progress.

This pragmatic view assumes that both treatments are effective and that the combination will have a positive interaction, additive, and perhaps synergistic.

MODELS FOR ANALYZING DRUG-PSYCHOTHERAPY INTERACTIONS

Reviewing the historical arguments with their ideological presumptions has facilitated an analysis of the claims and counterclaims into specific models. I have taken the analytic position that the ideological groups were hypothesizing possible mechanisms of drug-psychotherapy interactions, and I have thus far identified 13 models, each embodying an hypothesis asserted as fact by the conflicting groups.

Possible Negative Effects of Drug Therapy on Psychotherapy

Interestingly, most attention has been paid to the possible negative effects on psychotherapy caused by the introduction of drug therapy. Although relatively little empirical research has been done on this problem, it is possible to identify four proposed models (Figures 1, 2 and 3).

Model 1: *The negative placebo effect* (Figure 1). Much of the criticism of drug therapy enunciated by psychotherapists in the 1950s implied a negative placebo effect. It was claimed that the prescription of any drug had deleterious effects on the psychotherapeutic relationship and on the attitudes and behavior of both patient and therapist —effects independent of the specific pharmacologic actions of the

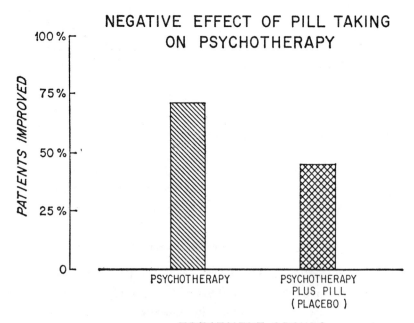

FIGURE 1. Models 1 and 4.

DRUG – INDUCED REDUCTION OF DISTRESS
REDUCES MOTIVATION FOR PSYCHOTHERAPY

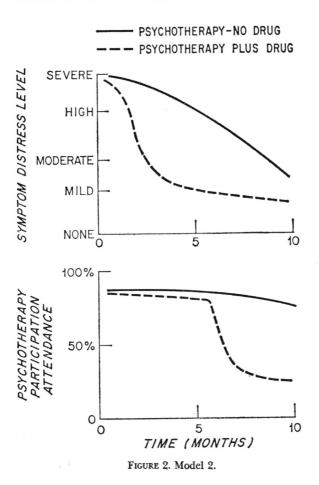

FIGURE 2. Model 2.

drug. Moreover, the prescription of medication promoted an authoritarian attitude on the part of the psychiatrist and enhanced a belief
in a biological-medical heritage. At the same time, the patient became
more dependent and assumed a more passive, compliant role as is
expected in the conventional doctor-patient relationship in fields of
medicine other than psychiatry. Thus, in this model the introduction

DRUGS UNDERMINE DEFENSES

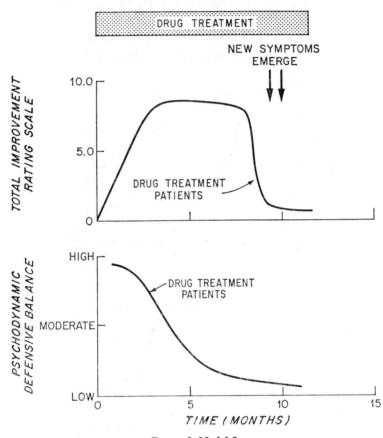

Figure 3. Model 3.

of medication into the psychotherapeutic process is hypothesized as initiating and/or augmenting countertransference and transference processes that run counter to the development of insight and the uncovering of defenses.

Model 2: *Drug-induced reduction of anxiety and symptoms as a motive for discontinuing psychotherapy* (Figure 2). In contrast to the negative placebo-effect model, which deals only with the symbolic and psychological meaning of drug administration, this model acknowledges the pharmacologic and therapeutic actions of drugs but expresses concern that the resultant decrease of the patient's anxiety and tension will reduce his motivation for continued psychotherapeutic participation. If a psychoactive drug such as phenothiazine or diazepoxide derivative is highly effective in reducing psychotic turmoil, neurotic anxiety, or other symptoms, the patient's motivation for reflection, insight, and psychotherapeutic work will be lessened (Meerloo, 1955; Szasz, 1957).

Model 3: *Pharmacotherapy undercuts defenses* (Figure 3). This model assumes that the pharmacologic effect of a drug prematurely undercuts some important defenses, and symptom substitution or other compensatory mechanisms of symptom formation will ensue. For example, in psychotherapeutic practice, Seitz (1953) has reported instances of new symptom formation following hypnosis. Weiss (1944) cautioned against an overly rapid relief of the anxiety of the agoraphobic. This model assumes that symptoms maintain a balance between conflict and defenses, and that the "precipitous" reduction of anxiety, depression, or tension may upset this equilibrium and release deeper conflicts.

Model 4: *Possible deleterious effects of pharmacotherapy on psychotherapy expectation* (Figure 1). This model assumes that there may be a negative reaction among some patients for whom drug therapy instead of psychotherapy is prescribed. Such patients may feel that the prescription of a drug defines them as "less interesting," and as unsuitable candidates for insight. Thus, the psychiatrist's prescription of drugs may trigger loss of the patients' self-esteem, especially if they belong to a cultural subgroup that values insight, psychotherapeutic understanding, and self-actualization. This expectation varies with the social class and subculture in which the patient participates. Within groups that value psychotherapy, the use of drugs is often regarded as a "failure" or "crutch."

Possible Positive Effects of Drug Therapy on Psychotherapy

The four models mentioned above illustrate only negative influences of drugs on the psychotherapeutic process. Although the possible negative influences have been given greatest attention by

DRUGS FACILITATE ACCESSIBILITY
TO PSYCHOTHERAPY

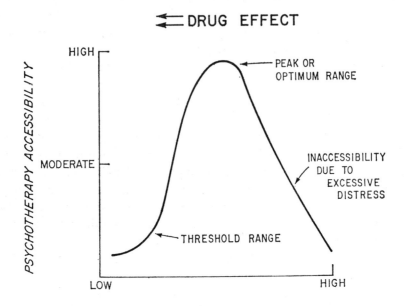

FIGURE 4. Model 5.

psychotherapeutic clinicians, a comprehensive analysis must give equal consideration to the ways in which drug therapy may facilitate, augment, and interact in a synergistic manner with psychotherapy and other therapies. At least six such models may be identified (Figures 4-9).

Model 5: *Drugs facilitate psychotherapeutic accessibility* (Figure 4). This model embodies the most commonly stated rationale for the use of combined therapies and supports prevailing clinical practice in psychiatry. The pharmacologic action of the drugs ameliorates the presumed CNS dysfunction underlying symptom formation, resulting in a reduction of the patient's symptoms and/or affective discomfort and rendering the patient better able to communicate in and benefit

DRUGS INFLUENCE PSYCHOLOGICAL FUNCTIONS NECESSARY
FOR PSYCHOTHERAPY PARTICIPATION

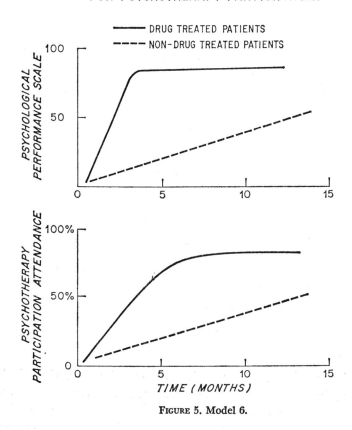

FIGURE 5. Model 6.

from psychotherapy. While some level of anxiety, dysphoria, or symp-tomatology is believed necessary to provide the "drive" or "motiva-tion" for participation in psychotherapy, this hypothesis presumes that excessive levels of tension, anxiety, or symptom intensity result in a decrease in the patient's capacity to participate effectively in psychotherapy.

Model 6: *Drugs influence the psychological functions required for participation in psychotherapy* (Figure 5) . This model is closely re-lated to the accessibility model and predicts that, through their action

DRUGS PROMOTE ABREACTION

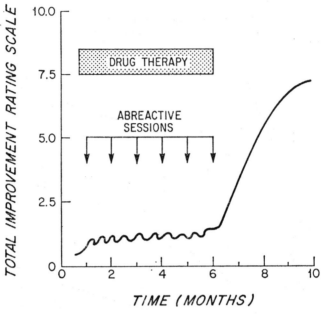

FIGURE 6. Model 7.

on neurophysiological substrates, drugs may enhance verbal skills, improve cognitive functioning and memory, reduce distraction, and promote attention and concentration. Since it is widely accepted that adequate psychological functioning is a prerequisite for psychotherapeutic participation, any improvement in these functions and abilities enhances the patient's benefit from participation in psychotherapy.

Model 7: *Drugs promote abreaction* (Figure 6). Abreaction is one of the earliest described psychotherapeutic techniques. Breuer and Freud (1950) in their early studies of hysteria reported on their use of hypnosis to promote catharsis or abreaction. A number of drugs, especially intravenous barbiturates and amphetamines, have been used to promote this effect. In his monograph on the pharmacologic basis of psychiatric therapy, Wikler (1957) referred to such methods

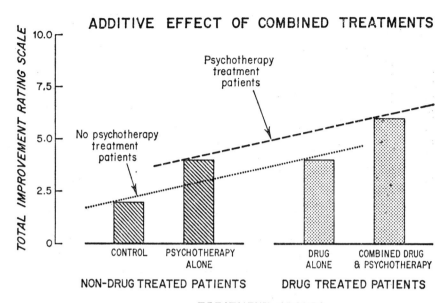

FIGURE 7. Model 9.

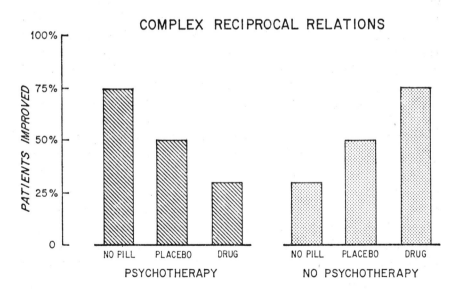

FIGURE 8. Model 10a.

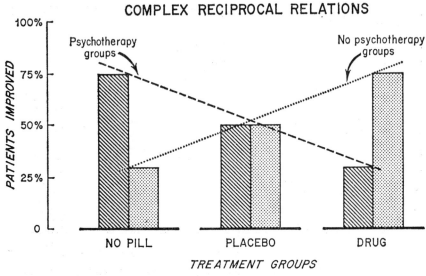

FIGURE 9. Model 10b.

as "psychoexploratory" techniques. These drugs help to uncover memory, break down defenses, and bring into consciousness material against which the person otherwise defends. A variant of this effort is the recent use of LSD, mescaline, and psilocybin to promote "peak experiences" in which the heightened sense of self-awareness and emotional, affective, and bodily experiences that occur under these psychedelic drugs are advocated as facilitating the psychotherapeutic process.

Model 8: *Positive placebo effect of drug therapy.* In addition to the short-term symptomatic relief of drug therapy, a positive placebo effect may contribute to the patient's optimism and confidence. The advocates of such popular biological methods as the megavitamin treatment for schizophrenia are indirectly removing some of the stigma from psychiatric illness and, in some instances, making it easier for the patient to accept the definition of himself as mentally ill. Thus, the request for drug therapy may be a vehicle through which the patient seeks psychotherapeutic help and counseling. (There is no graph representing this model.)

Model 9: *Additive effects of combined drugs and psychotherapy*

(Figure 7). Most practitioners presume that drugs alone and psychotherapy alone are ineffective. Advocates of combined therapy, however, assume some form of simple additive effects and believe psychotherapy alone or drug therapy alone would be equivalent.

Model 10: *Complex reciprocal relationship* (Figures 8 and 9). The most complex and sophisticated argument assumes that both the proponents and critics of drug therapy are correct, but that the nature of the drug effect will vary according to whether or not the patients are in psychotherapy. For patients who are not in psychotherapy, the drug effect will be positive and there will be a combination of active drug effect plus a positive placebo effect.

In the presence of psychotherapy, however, there will be a negative placebo effect and the opposite hierarchy of therapeutic effects will occur, so that patients in psychotherapy do best without any pill at all. An active drug, particularly one with sedative-hypnotic effects, would diminish the value of drug-psychotherapy combinations; not only would there be the negative placebo effect of pill-taking per se, but the active drug would decrease alertness, reduce verbal facility and memory, and impair the psychological functions necessary for psychotherapeutic participation.

Effects of Psychotherapy on Pharmacotherapy

Most of the discussion in the literature has focused on effects of drug therapy on psychotherapy. Less attention has been paid to the impact of psychotherapy on pharmacotherapy.

During discussions in the 1950s and 1960s, psychotherapists were the assertive parties to the dialogue and drug therapists were on the defensive. Today the impact of evidence from controlled studies has resulted in a subtle but significant shift. Considering the demonstrated efficacy of drugs for the treatment of depression and the absence of evidence for the efficacy of psychotherapy, the question has been raised: What benefit accrues to the depressed patient from psychotherapy added to drug therapy? At least three proposed models can be identified (Figures 10, 11 and 12).

Model 11: *Psychotherapy may be symptomatically disruptive* (Figure 10). Some pharmacotherapists hypothesize that psychotherapy

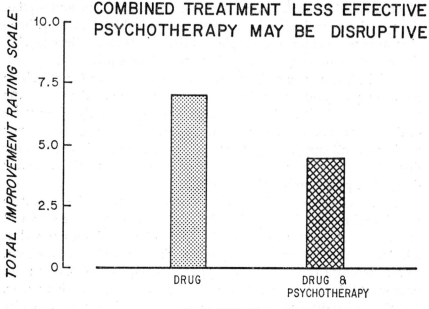

FIGURE 10. Model 11.

may be deleterious to pharmacologic treatment since symptoms may be aggravated by excessive probing and uncovering of defenses. Some psychiatrists who have worked with depressed and schizophrenic patients believe that psychotherapeutic intervention is harmful, particularly during the acute stage, and that during the early recovery process the patient is best left alone to "heal over" and to reconstitute his/her defenses. The fear hypothesized by pharmacotherapists is that psychotherapy, by uncovering areas of conflict, will increase the levels of tension. Implicit in this controversy is the variable of timing: What are the appropriate points at which primarily supportive psychotherapy should be pursued or probing insight techniques are indicated?

Model 12: *Biochemical replacement effect of drugs* (Figure 11). Some biological psychiatrists compare psychotropic drug treatment to non-psychiatric use of drugs in medicine, especially to the adminis-

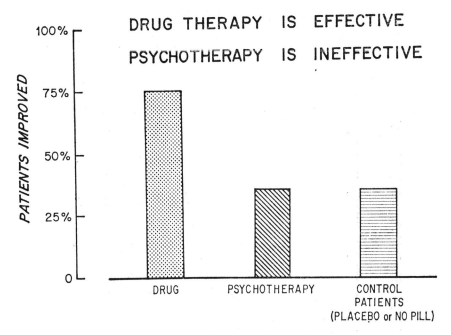

FIGURE 11. Model 12.

tration of endocrine agents like insulin for diabetes. For those who hold this view, the rectification by drugs of the presumed neurophysiological dysfunction or biochemical deficiency is the critical therapeutic factor, and psychotherapy is considered unnecessary and irrelevant or, at best, neutral. A variation of this reductionist, single-factor hypothesis is expressed by some proponents of lithium treatment for mania. The most extreme version is proposed by the advocates of megavitamin therapy for schizophrenia.

Model 13: *Psychotherapy as rehabilitation* (Figure 12). Most drug therapists value psychotherapy, but in a secondary and ameliorative way. They propose that psychotherpy does not act on etiological mechanisms or on the core of the depressive process but corrects secondary difficulties in interpersonal relations, in self-esteem, and in the psychological functions that follow the impact of depressive

DRUG TREATMENT IS PRIMARY
PSYCHOTHERAPY IS REHABILITATIVE

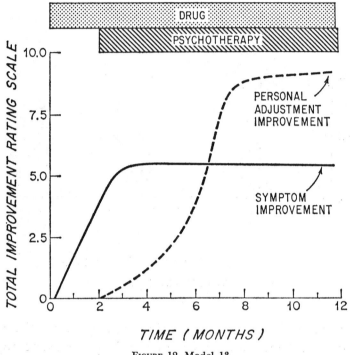

TIME (MONTHS)

FIGURE 12. Model 13.

symptoms. In this hypothesis, psychotherapy is seen as rehabilitative rather than therapeutic in the classical medical model. As such, it would be a purely elective rather than necessary component of the treatment program.

CONCLUSIONS

The combination of drugs and psychotherapy in psychiatric treatment is widely used but inadequately understood. Data from controlled trials are necessary to clarify the therapeutic issues. These issues are evident in the treatment of depression in which drugs and psychotherapy can be related to well specified, although only partially validated, theoretical models—the neurochemical models that explain and justify drug treatment and the psychodynamic models that underlie psychotherapeutic methods. Depression, therefore, presents one area of psychiatry that is theoretically active and therapeutically successful and where linkages between theory, experiment, and practice are emerging.

The data available from controlled studies demonstrate no negative interactions between drugs and psychotherapy for depression. On the contrary, there are probably synergistic effects because of the different processes that influence the two treatments. Psychotherapy influences interpersonal relations and social performance while drug therapy reduces symptom formation and affective distress. There are, moreover, sequential interactions such that sustained symptom reduction seems a necessary condition for the efficacy of psychotherapy.

There is relatively good evidence for the rejection of Models 1 and 8 that postulate either a negative or positive placebo effect (Luborsky, Singer, and Luborsky, 1975).

Model 5, which postulates that drugs render the patient more accessible to psychotherapy, is the one model most clearly supported by the data. Drug therapy contributes to a general attitude of optimism and confidence on the part of the therapist and the patient. This stems from the evidence that, with drug therapy, symptom control is feasible and the fear of a relapse reduced. Drug effect on symptom reduction is consistent with the fact that there are biochemical actions of drugs that rectify some CNS abnormality in the patient (Model 12) or reduce stress and render the patient more accessible to psychotherapeutic intervention and improved psychosocial coping (Group for Advancement of Psychiatry, 1975).

Furthermore, there is no evidence for the hypotheses that drug-induced reduction of symptoms is a motive for discontinuing psychotherapy (Model 2), that pharmacotherapy undercuts defenses (Model 3), that there is a possible deleterious effect of pharmacotherapy on psychotherapeutic expectation (Model 4), that drugs have an abreactive effect on the patient (Model 7), or that psychotherapy may be symptomatically disruptive (Model 11) (Weissman et al., 1974).

The model proposing that psychotherapy is rehabilitative (Model

13) is consistent with the presented evidence, but alternative interpretations are possible. There is insufficient evidence either way for
the model showing that drugs influence the psychological functions
required for participation in psychotherapy (Model 6) (Greenblatt,
1975).

Further conceptual analyses are needed not only for the psychodynamic psychotherapy discussed in this paper but for the inclusion
of other aspects of psychotherapy, particularly those forms that attempt to influence more enduring personality structures and the
presumed vulnerability to react to stress with affective symptom-
atology.

Unfortunately, in the development of a scientific basis for psychiatry, clinical practices are still ahead of systematic investigations.
In most therapeutic decisions, pragmatic experience more often
guides the psychiatrist than does evidence from systematic clinical
trials, experimental studies on animals, or basic laboratory findings.

The treatment of depression thus serves as only one example of
a compartmentalized and fragmented state of contemporary theory
and practice. In building a scientific psychiatry, the issues raised by
the treatment of depression with combined drugs and psychotherapy
apply equally to treatment of other clinical psychiatric states, and
most of the problems described in this paper are only specific illustra-
tions of general problems in psychiatric therapeutics.

REFERENCES

AZIMA, H. 1961. Psychodynamic and psychotherapeutic problems in connection with
    imipramine (Tofranil) intake. *Journal of Mental Science*, 107:74-82.
BELLAK, L. and ROSENBERG, S. 1966. Effects of antidepressant drugs on psychodynamics.
    Psychosomatics, 7:106-114.
BREUER, J. and FREUD, S. 1950. *Studies in Hysteria*. Boston: Beacon Press.
COVI, L., LIPMAN, R. S., DEROGATIS, L. R., SMITH, J. E., III, and PATTISON, J. H. 1974.
    Drugs and group psychotherapy in neurotic depression. *Am. J. Psychiatry*, 131:
    191-198.
FIEVE, R. R. 1975. *Mood Swings: The Third Revolution in Psychiatry*. New York:
    William Morrow.
FRIEDMAN, A. S. 1975. Drugs and family therapy in the treatment of depression. *Arch.
    Gen. Psychiatry*, 32:619-637.
GOTTSCHALK, L. A., GLESER, G. C., WYLIE, H. W., JR., and KAPLAN, S. M. 1965. Effects
    of imipramine on anxiety and hostility levels. *Psychopharmacologia*, 7:303-310.
GREENBLATT, M. (ed.) 1975. *Drugs in Combination with Other Therapies. Seminars in
    Psychiatry*. New York: Grune & Stratton.

Group for the Advancement of Psychiatry (GAP). 1975. *Pharmacotherapy and Psychotherapy: Paradoxes, Problems, and Progress.* New York: GAP, Vol. 9, Report no. 93, March.

HOLLINGSHEAD, A. B. and REDLICH, F. C. 1958. *Social Class and Mental Illness.* New York: John Wiley & Sons.

KLERMAN, G. L. and GERSHON, S. 1970. Imipramine effects upon hostility in depression. *J. Nerv. Ment. Dis.,* 150:127-132.

KLERMAN, G. L., DiMASCIO, A., WEISSMAN, M., PRUSOFF, B., and PAYKEL, E. S. 1974. Treatment of depression by drugs and psychotherapy. *Am. J. Psychiatry,* 131:186-191.

KLINE, N. S. 1974. *From Sad to Glad.* New York: Putnam.

KRAMER, M., WHITMAN, R., BALDRIDGE, B., and ORNSTEIN, P. H. 1968. Drugs and dreams: III. The effects of imipramine on the dreams of depressed patients. *Am. J. Psychiatry,* 124:1385-1392.

LEWINSOHN, P. M. 1974. A behavioral approach to depression. In R. J. Friedman and M. M. Katz (eds.), *The Psychology of Depression: Contemporary Theory and Research.* Washington, D.C.: Hemisphere Publications.

LUBORSKY, L., SINGER, B., and LUBORSKY, L. 1975. Comparative studies of psychotherapies. *Arch. Gen. Psychiatry,* 32:995-1008.

McLEAN, P. 1975. Behavior therapy. Presented to the Society for Psychotherapy Research, panel on "Outcome Studies of Depression." Boston, Massachusetts, June 12.

MEERLOO, J. A. M. 1955. Medication into submission: The danger of therapeutic coercion. *J. Nerv. Ment. Dis.,* 122:353-360.

OSTOW, M. 1967. *Drugs in Psychoanalysis and Psychotherapy.* New York: Basic Books.

RUSH, A. J. 1975. Cognitive therapy vs. pharmacotherapy. Presented to the Society for Psychotherapy Research, panel on "Outcome Studies of Depression." Boston, Massachusetts, June 12.

SARWER-FONER, M. S. 1960. *The Dynamics of Psychiatric Drug Therapy.* Springfield, Ill.: Charles C Thomas.

SEITZ, P. F. 1953. Experiments in the substitution of symptoms by hypnosis. *Psychosom. Med.,* 15:405-424.

SHAW, B. 1975. Cognitive therapy vs. behavior therapy. Presented to the Society for Psychotherapy Research, panel on "Outcome Studies of Depression." Boston, Massachusetts, June 12.

SZASZ, T. S. 1957. Some observations on the use of tranquilizing drugs. *A. M. A. Archives of Neurology and Psychiatry,* 77:86-92.

WEISS, E. 1944. Clinical aspects of depression. *Psychoanal. Q.,* 13:445-461.

WEISSMAN, M. M., KLERMAN, G. L., PAYKEL, E. S., PRUSOFF, B., and HANSON, B. 1974. Treatment effects on the social adjustment of depressed patients. *Arch. Gen. Psychiatry,* 30:771-778.

WIKLER, A. 1957. *The Relation of Psychiatry to Pharmacology.* Baltimore: Williams & Wilkins.

6

Helping Alliances in Psychotherapy

LESTER LUBORSKY, Ph.D.

Most papers on what is variously termed "the helping alliance," "the therapeutic alliance," "the working alliance," or "the helping relationship" are either on the questions of what it is or how it relates to the outcome of treatment. Almost all the research is clinical and conceptual. I, too, shall start in this usual style (in part A), for it has been productive, and then go on to try a less usual clinical-quantitative combination (in part B).

A. WHAT IT IS

Reviewing the old terrain and staking it out according to a convenient "map" of some divisions in the process of psychotherapy (Figure 1), I find that the largest natural division of the process of psychotherapy is in its ends versus its means, the *goals* to be achieved versus the *means* to achieve them. For example, at the beginning of treatment the patient may tell the therapist, "My goal is to be rid of my depressions." The therapist may then suggest, "Okay, let's try psychotherapy as the means."

A briefer version of this paper was presented to the 1975 annual meeting of the Society for Psychotherapy Research in Boston.

Partial support for this study was provided by U.S. Public Health Service Research Grant MH 15442 and Research Scientist Award MH 40710 to Dr. Luborsky of the University of Pennsylvania, Department of Psychiatry, and Eastern Pennsylvania Psychiatric Institute. Dr. Ed Bordin's work in this area was the immediate impetus for the present paper; Marjorie Cohen and Paul Christoph assisted with its preparation.

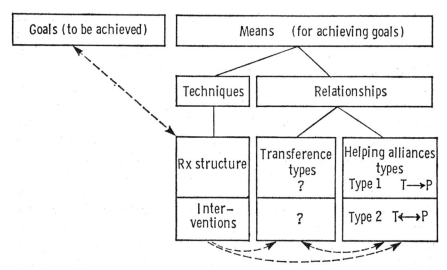

FIGURE 1. Diagram of the main means for achieving goals in psychoanalytically oriented psychotherapies.

The means in turn may be subdivided into another neat dichotomy: the *techniques* used and the *relationships* developed. This is the familiar dichotomy put forward by many writers; for example, Strupp (1973) concluded that there are two main classes of effective ingredients in the process of psychotherapy—the relationship established by the therapist by virtue of the therapist's qualities and the technical means and information that he uses.

The techniques are of two main kinds: the *treatment structure* itself and the specific *interventions* such as interpretations. The treatment structure includes the supportiveness versus expressiveness dimension, the degree of focus on the search for understanding, the degree of structure imposed by reference to specific goals.

The relationship box in Figure 1 is drawn larger than the technique box since it is considered the more crucial vehicle for achieving benefits from treatment. In fact, even the technique component of a search for understanding may provide much more than the value of the understanding itself—it may improve the working-alliance component of the relationship by offering both patient and therapist a common task on which they can collaborate.

And so we go on in the deliquescing tree of dichotomies in Figure 1 to the final major one. The relationship box can be resolved into at least two major branches: *transference types* and *helping relationship types*. There may be some value in distinguishing other kinds of relationship components but they do not seem nearly so important as a means for achieving goals in treatment. The transference qualities are defined by Curtis (1973) according to a usual definition that combines both clinical and metapsychological considerations: "Transference is a revival in a current object relationship, especially to the analyst, of thought, feeling and behavior derived from repressed fantasies originating in significant conflictual childhood relationships." The transference component and the helping-alliance component are often opposed to each other, although they need not always be opposed, since at times the transference, especially the positive transference, grooves with the growth of the helping alliance.

Two main types of helping alliance may be distinguished, following partly the conceptualization of Greenspan and Cullander (1975):

Type 1: A therapeutic alliance based on the patient's experiencing the therapist as supportive and helpful with himself as the recipient.

Type 2: A therapeutic alliance based on a sense of working together in a joint struggle against what is impeding the patient. The emphasis here is on shared responsibility for working out the treatment goals. When this is present, the alliance qualities of the relationship are evident in a sense of "we-ness." The transition to a Type 2 helping alliance is often clearest when termination begins to be a possibility. Then the patient frequently articulates fears about the difficulty in carrying on without the direct help of the therapist. The best fruit of this discussion is for the patient to recognize that he can carry on the operations the two of them have done together. In a beneficially developing treatment the patient usually will have realized that what he does is in part similar to what the therapist does, that is, to listen and then understand so that, in a real sense, the jobs of patient and therapist have basic similarities. This fact further promotes a sense of conjoint activity.

The strength of the working alliance may be judged by: 1) its capacity to withstand stress under pressure from regressive developments (usually based on increased transference) versus its readiness to break down with minor frustrations; 2) the degree of dedication to and persistence in the work of treatment to overcome obstacles in oneself.

The strength of the helping alliances varies from time to time, especially in relation to surges in transference which may then be diminished by the therapist's interventions. As Freud suggested, one must pay special attention to that part of transference that might interfere with the positive transference, and not make one's communication to the patient before a "proper rapport" has been established (Freud, 1913, p. 139). The therapist's interventions are not only aimed directly at modulating the transference when it gets in the way, but at improving the helping relationship so that it can tolerate surges of transference. As Zetzel (1958) suggested:

> If the analyst can actively convey his participation and partnership with the patient as a real person, development of a secure working relationship—the therapeutic alliance—will be encouraged (p. 190).

She believed that the analyst, as the transference neurosis develops, must show the patient a distinction between his fantasies and the real relationship. In Figure 1, the arrow from the "treatment structure" to the "goals" is intended to suggest that the reference to goals themselves may be used as another important intervention; it may minimize transference developments and cement the helping alliance, especially each time a phase in the goals has been achieved. Similarly, Rogers (1961) suggests ways the therapist can try to create a helping relationship; foremost is to be perceived by the patient as trustworthy, dependable, and consistent.

In sum, the helping alliance can be defined broadly, as it often is defined, to include aspects of "the goals, techniques and bonds" suggested by Bordin (1975). It may, however, be defined more specifically as in Figure 1 by limiting it to Type 1 and Type 2 helping relationships, especially the latter.

A Clinical Example of Helping Relationships and Related Concepts

A brief clinical vignette will help to illustrate the concepts in my map of the means and ends in the psychotherapeutic process.

Therapist's notes on the patient based on the first session:

The patient was referred by a psychiatrist friend, Dr. R. She has had previous psychotherapy with Dr. J and with Dr. C. She broke off therapy with Dr. C because she was angry that he used some of her time to ask her questions about furnishing his house. He also suggested some men for her to meet, and she felt that she can get these kinds of suggestions from her friends. He also made some wild interpretations such as "I can't give you a penis."

The patient is unhappy because she is involved in a hopeless situation with a married man. Four years ago her husband was in an automobile accident which led to the discovery that he was keeping a 20-year-old girl in an apartment. There was a separation, and her husband went to Nevada to avoid paying support to her and the children. They got divorced about one and one-half years ago, and she received an adequate settlement. He subsequently married his mistress, and they have a baby. She became involved with a married man, M, who was the husband of a friend of hers. She knew her friend had been having affairs and had been intending to get a divorce. Since the patient began her affair with M, his wife has changed her mind, and the patient shows disappointment. From time to time M has qualms of conscience and tries to break off the relationship. Whenever this happens, the patient feels very unhappy, cries, and tries to find someone to tell her miseries to. Whenever she sees M, she seems to be happy.

The patient also has a phobia for driving over high bridges and for driving by herself to the ski resorts. Her latest disappointment occurred after she had phoned M to go skiing and learned that he had already arranged to go skiing with a male friend.

The patient is the youngest child of three. She has a sister 12 years older and a brother 10 years older. When she was about 20 years old her father was run over by a bus and died. Her mother remained depressed for nine years, and the patient stayed at home and took care of her mother without much help from her brother or sister. She supported herself as a piano teacher. Her mother developed arteriosclerosis, gangrene of the leg, and had to have an amputation. It was about that time that the patient had broken off the engagement with her husband because she felt he was dull and not the kind of man she wanted. He was very kind and helped with the care of the mother until the mother died. The patient married him with a feeling of gratitude. Her husband was in the building business, and their income was sporadically good or bad. She finally helped him get a good start by using her savings and borrowing money from members of her family. He is now very successful.

The couple had a sterility problem which was supposedly due to her husband's low sperm count. They were able to adopt two boys now 13 and 11. After the patient separated from her husband, she became an interior decorator and is now fairly successful. About one and a half years ago she became pregnant by M, but because of her situation had a therapeutic abortion. She wanted to prove she was a woman and could get pregnant and regretted not being in a situation where she could have kept the baby.

Her purpose in seeking further psychiatric treatment is to be able to be happy, but she is uncertain how she can be helped by seeing a psychiatrist. It seems that she has a need for someone to talk to. At the end of the interview, she commented that the doctor had narrow feet and associated to the idea that M's feet are narrow and her husband's feet are broad. She also thought that the doctor's shoes were not new, and this meant that he was not vain. Her husband was vain.

She and M have common interests in art and music. She thinks he would make an ideal husband and does not know whether she should break off with him because she is so unhappy or whether she should try harder to get him to separate from his wife. The patient is being referred to the psychotherapy research study. She agreed to take the tests and have her future psychotherapeutic sessions tape-recorded. She was flattered by the offer because it made her feel like a special person. It reminded her of an occasion when a photographer took her picture at a ski resort because he liked her costume.

Post-therapy sketch by interviewer for psychotherapy research project:

The patient has clearly developed a style of life which largely satisfies her; this has occurred during the time that she has been in therapy, and she attributes most of the changes to therapy without much idea how therapy resulted in these changes. She appears to be managing her own business and her household quite successfully. Her image of herself seems to be much more positive now, and she is much less subject to periods of depression. She also seems to be much less phobic than when she began therapy.

She still impresses me as quite superficial, full of petty complaints. Although she does not have any current prospects for remarriage, she seems to have a number of friends of both sexes. There does seem to be a significant lack of concern for other people—none of her talks of friends or of her children gave much of a sense of depth of involvement with them. In general, however, I would have to consider this a very successful treatment and I suspect that she will continue at this level.

Some of my observations based on the early and late sessions.

In the early sessions the patient was tremendously worried about herself. She kept asking about whether the therapist had received the report of the psychological tests from the psychotherapy research project because she felt that there was something terribly wrong with her, and she wanted the therapist to "tell me I'm all right." Even in the third session she made it plain that she wanted to give up M. She began to date, and in session five even began to "feel better about not seeing M." She even stopped taking tranquilizers. These seem to be early indications of the beginning development of a Type 1 helping relationship.

In the later sessions, just after the therapist's vacation, she quit her job because she felt she was not getting enough recognition as "the number one saleswoman." Yet in the ensuing interaction with the therapist she managed to convey to him that she was in fact managing very well and making more money now in her own business than she had before. There was a considerable increase in confidence in herself and in her relationship to the therapist. She felt that she had awareness about herself which the therapist should respect. This might be the beginning of a Type 2 helping relationship. A follow-up after five years and a brief interview with the therapist revealed that the patient had maintained her gains despite having to deal with a severe physical problem that had developed.

B: How Can Helping Relationships (and Other Relationship Patterns) Be Measured and How Are They Related to Outcome?

The broader research area in psychology in which the phenomena of helping alliances fit is referred to often as "human attraction" (Huston, 1974; Byrne, 1971). Within psychotherapy research, Barrett-Lennard's relationship questionnaire (1962) given to the patient (and therapist) at the end of the fifth session probably estimates, in part, facets of helping relationships. His measure is predictive of treatment outcome, especially for the patients' forms. Ryan's study (1973) on the capacity to enter a therapeutic relationship is most similar to my approach. Indices of hope (based on independent interviews) and indices of object relations (based on early memories) were related to the strength of the "working alliance" as shown at the start of treatment.

I wrote all of part A before becoming burdened by inspecting any systematic collection of data. After rereading it, it seemed to me time to add to the familiar clinical concept-generating attitude a relentless psychologist's "show-me" attitude. Two points needed to be shown: 1) that one can recognize these types of helping relationships both by ratings and by scoring systems, 2) that helping relationships are related to the outcomes of treatment. Two specific propositions about outcomes needed to be especially examined: 1) More successful treatments will show earlier and greater development of helping relationships; 2) the Type 2 helping relationship is a more substantial achievement than the Type 1 helping relationship, and it therefore will be of more lasting value to the patient.

I shall now give some of the history of my long search for the curative factors in psychotherapy that led me to the two propositions. In the Penn Psychotherapy Research Project (Auerbach, Luborsky, and Johnson, 1972; Luborsky and Mintz, in preparation), the initial characteristics of the patient and of the therapist predicted only a small part of the variance of outcomes. The only other large multivariate predictive study came to the same conclusion (Fiske, Cartwright, and Kirtner, 1964). Even the match of patients' and therapists' characteristics predicted little of the variance.

Maybe certain *types* of psychotherapy are especially curative. A review of comparative treatment studies for different psychotherapies (Luborsky, Singer, and Luborsky, 1975) showed that the designated type of treatment generally had little differential impact on the numbers of patients benefiting from these treatments.

Although the majority of patients benefit from psychotherapy, it is clear that the outcome of *each* treatment venture is only slightly predictable from the initial characteristics of the patient, the therapist, the match of the patient and therapist (as evaluated *before* treatment), and the treatment type. Since initial characteristics contribute only slightly to the prediction of outcome, one hopes for a beneficial interaction of patient and therapist to emerge as treatment proceeds. Carl Rogers' opinion (personal communication) of about 20 years ago seems confirmed, that the treatment venture is an "adventure."

The hoped-for beneficial interactions, we began to surmise, might have as its groundwork a major common ingredient in different forms of psychotherapy—the quality of the helping relationship established (Luborsky, Singer, and Luborsky, 1975). To understand that groundwork I began to work out ways of delineating the main relationship themes described or enacted in treatment so that I could track the development of the types of helping relationships and see how these related to the types of conflictual relationships. What follows are the details of how this task was accomplished.

Procedures

Three main types of procedures were necessary: for selecting more- versus less-improved patients; for developing methods to evaluate the strength of the different types of helping relationships; and to evaluate the conflictual-relationship themes. For all three procedures I was guided by the principle of parsimony, that is, to find the simplest possible procedure for reducing the complex data.

1. *Selection of extreme groups: more- versus less-improved patients.* The tape recordings of the psychoanalytically oriented psychotherapy* of the 73 patients in the Penn Psychotherapy Research

---

* Only three were formal psychoanalyses.

Project were the data base (almost all were in the neurotic range). Rather than transcribing and reading transcripts for all patients, focusing on small extreme groups seemed much more feasible. The ten most improved and the ten least improved of the 73 patients were selected on the two most reasonable outcome measures: "residual gain" and "rated change." It is the first that will be used mainly in the present report.

Residual gain is a composite of measures provided by the patient and by the clinical observer initially and at termination (with the patient measures and clinical-observer measures weighted equally). It is a component of the difference between composite measures, initially and at termination, with the gain scaled relative to other patients starting at the same initial level. It correlated .76 with rated change. Another way to describe residual gain is that it is that part of the "raw" gain which is not linearly predictable from pretreatment adjustment level.

Rated change is a combination of ratings of change made by patient and therapist independently, each weighted equally. Since substantial agreement existed between patients' and therapists' ratings—something that has not been typical in other studies—a combined measure could be obtained. This outcome measure, rated change, actually correlated highly (.68) with the raw gain, that is, the difference between pre- and post-treatment adjustment scores. (Within the more- and less-improved subgroups, especially for the rated change criterion, patients may start at somewhat different levels and, therefore, the process may be different.)

The patients in each extreme group were markedly different not only in outcome according to our main criterion, residual gain, but also for the other measures—therapists' ratings, patients' ratings, and clinical observers' ratings, as well as on the reasons for termination as stated by the therapist (Tables 1 and 2). The mean number of sessions was only slightly greater for the high improvers. For the present report, we further restricted the extreme groups of ten each to those patients who had at least 25 sessions, since our main interest was in intensive treatment. For the residual-gain criterion there were seven high-gain patients and eight low- or no-gain patients. For the

TABLE 1

Ten Patients who Made Most Improvement Among 73
(Penn Psychotherapy Project)

Ranked on Residual Gain

Rank	Patient No.	Sex	T Ratings	P Satisfaction	O Improvement	No. of Sessions	Reason for Termination
1	45	F	7, 7, 7	6.5	4	39	mostly patient's initiative
2	18	F	8, 7, 7	8	4	56	nat., at patient's initiative
3	49	F	8, 7, 7	8	5	99	nat., at patient's initiative
4	68	M	9, 7, 8	9	4	8 or 9	nat., at patient's initiative
5	27	M	7, 7, 7	7.5	4, 4.5	98	nat.
6	7	M	7, 7, 7	9	4	10	short-term goals achieved
7	60	F	7, 8, 7	7.5	3.5, 4	13	nat., at patient's initiative
8	71	F	7.5, 7, 8	9	4	88	nat., by patient & therapist
9	53	F	9, 9, 8	8	5/2	290	nat., mutual
10	17	F	7, 7, 7	9	4	65	almost terminated; hospitalized with hepatitis
	Means		7.7, 7.3, 7.3	8.2	4.2	77	

T Ratings = ratings by therapist at termination (1-9 scale) on three similar improvement scales
P Satisfaction = rating by patient at termination (1-9 scale)
O Improvement = rating of improvement by observer at termination (1-5 scale)

TABLE 2

Ten Patients Who Made Least Improvement Among 73
(Penn Psychotherapy Project)

Ranked on Residual Gain

Rank	Patient No.	Sex	T Ratings	P Satisfaction	O Improvement	No. of Sessions	Reason for Termination
1	46	M	5, 5, 6	3	2.1	21	patient moving
2	94	F	3, 3, 6	4.5	2.5	31	therapist leaving
3	6	F	4, 6, 6	4	1.1	46	against advice
4	63	F	8, 2, 9	4	2	27	against advice
5	81	F	3, 3, 5	1.5	2	40+	at parents' instigation
6	52	M	4, 2, 6	4.5	3	264	against advice
7	101	M	3, 4, 5	2	1.5	30	went to different therapist
8	5	F	8, 7, 6	8	3	52	therapist leaving; extraneous factor
9	77	M	2, 1, 5	2	2	85	against advice
10	85	M	8, 7, 6	8	2	15	patient moved
Means			4.8, 4.0, 6.0	4.2	2.1	61.1	

T Ratings = ratings by therapist at termination (1-9 scale)
P Satisfaction = rating by patient at termination (1-9 scale)
O Improvement = rating of improvement by observer at termination (1-5 scale)

rated change extreme groups there were eight and seven patients in each. Six highs and seven lows were extremes by both criteria.

2. *Selection of sessions: early versus late sessions.* A sample of the sessions was reviewed and two early and two late sessions were selected for each patient. The two early sessions usually were sessions number 3 and 5; the two late sessions were the one at the 90 percent completion of treatment and the prior session.

It seemed sufficient to use the first 20 minutes of the sessions studied as a way of reducing the amount of data. The first 20 minutes seemed preferable to a random middle segment, since by using this method, the reader would know everything that happened in the session up to the end of the sample.

3. *Steps for scoring the strength of the types of helping relationships.* Largely on the basis of clinical experience, a list of signs of each type of helping relationship was composed (Appendix A). Two judges independently read the four 20-minute segments for a subsample of patients, noting all instances of these signs. One of the two judges (Dr. Tom Wolman) did not know whether the patient was an improver or non-improver, and whether the session was early or late. Agreement was moderate.*

4. *Steps in determining the core conflictual-relationship theme.* The beginning and end of each relationship episode were first noted on the transcripts of the 20-minute segments. The episodes were usually identifiable and separable, although often they could also be seen as subepisodes of larger ones. Focusing on these episodes reduced the data, and more importantly, it highlighted relationship behaviors that were of most interest. The relationship episodes were those described as occurring outside the treatment setting and those actually engaged in with the therapist. Although my primary interest was in the helping relationships as portrayed in the conceptual map (Figure 1), I had wanted to identify the main relationship qualities to see how the helping relationships fit with the transference aspect of relationships. However, I did not believe that this small sample of sessions would be a safe basis for discerning transference patterns.

---

* Two other completely independent judges (Dr. Homer Curtis and Dr. Jack Solomon) are rating all patients in these groups and achieving high inter-judge agreement (Rose Morgan, Ph.D. thesis, in progress).

Although there is some evidence (Luborsky et al., 1973) that transference can be rated from small segments of sessions, the degree of agreement is not high and the relationship of such transference ratings to the clinically derived core transference patterns is difficult to verify. It seemed wiser, therefore, to cull the relationship episodes. In this first step, each clearly evident relationship episode is marked in the transcript and the clarity of the episode rated. The episodes were also identified in terms of the "object" they dealt with; for example, therapist, parents, spouse, or friends. (The focus around objects was also supported by an early study [Luborsky et al., 1973] of transference—transference *as expressed to particular objects* could be rated with more interjudge agreement than transference based on an entire segment.)

All relationship episodes regardless of type of object* were inspected in sequence to find thematic consistencies. This was done first for all relationship episodes in the first 20 minutes of the two early sessions, then done again in identical fashion for all relationship episodes in the later two sessions. The inspection job is a high-level clinical exercise; the key to finding the consistencies is reading and rereading the episodes. The earlier episodes become easier to understand after the later episodes are studied, redundant themes within and across episodes gradually appearing in a saltatorial sequence of eurekas. It does not matter that a few episodes are opaque or do not seem to fit; these drop out since the attention is only on repetitive themes. The redundancy of the theme marks the main conflict. (Luborsky [1976] gives more on the core conflictual relationship method.)

Working with such a reduced sample of data seemed at first like riding a bike with no hands—after all, the analyses of relationship patterns were being based only on the relationship episodes in four 20-minute samples for each patient's entire treatment. After more experience, the phenomenon being evaluated seemed so robust that I regarded the danger of serious spills as unlikely.

---

* If a larger number of episodes were surveyed, themes special to subclasses of objects *might* appear.

Table 3

Ten Patients Who Made Most Improvement Among 73
(Penn Psychotherapy Project)

Helping Alliance Signs

Rank	Patient No.	Helping Alliance Type 1		Helping Alliance Type 2	
		early session	*late session*	*early session*	*late session*
1	45	+ ?			
2	18	?			
3	49	+			+
4	68 X				
5	27	±	+		+
6	7 X				
7	60 X				
8	71	+ ?	+		
9	53	+			
10	17	+			

X = not included because there were fewer than 25 sessions.
+ = The scores are positive.
± = The scores are mostly positive.

Results and Discussion

Proposition 1. A sample of the early sessions will show the beginnings of helping relationships in the high improvers but not in the low improvers.

As Tables 3 and 4 demonstrate, the difference was striking—helping relationships developed with six of the seven improvers and none of the eight nonimprovers. In fact, all of the eight nonimprovers showed mainly negative helping relationship signs. According to our scoring manual, this means that the high improvers, by statements in sessions 3 and 5, reflected actual benefits or began to expect benefits from the therapeutic relationship. The benefits were only slight—a slight gain toward achieving a goal, an improvement in the relationship with the therapist, or a newly acquired awareness. For example:

Patient 49, session 5: "I was beginning to feel better about not seeing M, too." (This is an aim with which the patient started treatment.)

TABLE 4

Ten Patients Who Made Least Improvement Among 73
(Penn Psychotherapy Project)

Helping Alliance Signs

Rank	Patient No.	Helping Alliance Type 1		Helping Alliance Type 2	
		early session	late session	early session	late session
1	46 X				
2	94	—			
3	6	±	—		
4	63	—			
5	81	—			
6	52	— ?			
7	101	—		—	
8	5	—			
9	77	—			
10	85 X				

X = not included because there were fewer than 25 sessions.
— = The scores are negative.
± = The scores are mostly negative.

Patient 71, session 17:* "I've been thinking about you . . . I guess ever since last week or a couple of weeks ago. I feel not so strange, you know. Not like we're strangers, something like that. I feel closer to you."

Thus the improvers began to report perceptions of making gains or expecting to make gains quite early in treatment. In the manual these are called signs of Type 1 helping relationships. They seemed to occur in patients who, according to evaluations at termination of treatment, eventually improved most. We may have discovered something like the predictors of success in college: The best predictor of final grades is early grades; that is, the best predictor of later benefits is signs of early benefits or expectations of early benefits expressed in the early sessions.

How should we understand this and try to use it? As I mentioned, benefits from psychotherapy are a function, only to a small extent, of the qualities of the patient. The qualities of the therapist, as measured outside of treatment, are even less predictive. One thera-

---

* The earliest session available for this patient.

pist had a patient who turned out in the improvers and another in the nonimprovers, a further illustration of the fact that good and poor therapists were fairly well distributed across the patient sample. Even the match of patient-therapist qualities, as I mentioned, is not very predictive, although there may be some unmeasured elements in the patient-therapist match that are important, those related to "hitting it off," "clicking," "mutual attraction," or whatever contributes to the helping relationship. As one possible application, one might try at an early stage of treatment to re-pair patients and therapists so that each of them could express preferences about each other. Such opportunities for trying other patient-therapist pairings rarely occur. Patients and therapists get locked in and try to work things out for better or for worse. Fortunately, it is usually for better—most patients improve—but one aim of my research is to try to make things better for those for whom it is not for the better and even, as Bergin (1970) shows, it is occasionally for the worse.

Proposition 2. A sample of the later sessions will show (Table 3) that some of the improvers develop Type 2 helping relationships while the nonimprovers do not (Table 4). Some examples:

Patient 49, session 89:

> P: Well, I, my, you know, I want to tell you something, Doctor Freud (laughs). Don't know why I said that.
> T: Dr. Freud?
> P: How'd you like that . . . well they both begin with "F."
> T: F-R-E as a matter of fact.
> P: That's right. See, you're just as aware of it as I am. More so. Want me to analyze that?

In this example the patient admires the therapist and feels they share an awareness and method in common.

Patient 27, session 62:

> P: . . . whenever I run into a situation that I want to sort out in my mind now, I have like a sort of another part of my mind that's sort of a fantasy of you and I'm talking to you in my mind and that just sort of happens like that and so I started to work things out . . . there's

> a dimension of objectivity. . . . I just noticed it that be-
> ginning, that type of thing really beginning about last
> summer.

The patient seems to be developing an identification with the therapist, especially with the observing function of the therapist.

Only a few improvers provide evidence for Type 2 helping relationships. Comparing those improvers who do with those who do
not would be valuable; especially valuable would be to study the
long-term follow-up, which is in progress, to see whether patients
who have improved *and* developed a Type 2 helping relationship
maintain their gains better than do improvers who have not developed such a relationship.

Proposition 3. A pervasive conflictual-relationship theme can be
abstracted which resembles the clinically derived transference pattern.

A core conflictual-relationship theme was extracted by a new
method, described above, and shown to be pervasive in the early
sessions. The same theme was found in the later sessions for both
improvers and nonimprovers. Nevertheless, late in treatment *both*
the improvers and nonimprovers developed a deeper involvement
and therefore experienced their conflictual theme directly in the relationship with the therapist.

What then is the difference between the high and low improvers
if the core conflictual-relationship theme is evident both early and
late? The main difference seems to be that the improvers were more
capable of coping with the theme when it was experienced in the
relationship, or even outside of the relationship. For example, Patient
49 started treatment with the sense that there was something catas-
trophically wrong with her which she could not manage on her own.
She ended treatment with a renewed sense of self-confidence although
the core conflictual-relationship theme was still present. Evidently
she became able to manage it. What made her better able to manage
it? We can speculate that it was because a helping relationship had
developed. This attractive conclusion requires further analyses which
I hope to provide in future reports. I hope also to examine types
of core conflictual-relationship themes to see whether these types
differ compared with the types of helping relationships. The core con-

flictual-relationship theme appears to be a stable psychic structure similar to the transference pattern, but building a firm bridge across the concepts remains a forbiddingly difficult job.

Proposition 4. The improvers seem to come to treatment with slightly more positive expectations from "objects," which may facilitate the formation of helping relationships. (The results appear to be confirmatory but are not yet complete.)

Proposition 5. The therapists of the improvers try harder to develop helping relationships. A simple manual was constructed to evaluate this type of therapist behavior (Appendix B). (The results appear to be confirmatory but are not yet complete.)

OVERVIEW

It is an innovation to take the valuable clinical concept of helping alliances, transform it into operational terms, and apply it to a sample of patients in psychotherapy whose outcomes have been measured independently.

The most striking finding is how early in treatment the improvers show evidence of Type 1 helping relationships. Only a few of these patients form Type 2 helping relationships.

A new method was devised so that a core conflictual-relationship theme could be identified. This same theme was found both early and late in treatment, but the improvers evidenced more signs of mastering the theme. Later analyses will explore the possibility that those who develop helping relationships already have more positive expectations from "objects" expressed in their core conflictual relationships.

REFERENCES

Auerbach, A., Luborsky, L., and Johnson, M. 1972. Clinicians' predictions of psychotherapy outcome: A trial of a prognostic index. *Am. J. Psychiatry,* 128:830-835.

Barrett-Lennard, G. T. 1962. Dimensions of therapist response as causal factors in therapeutic change. *Psychological Monographs,* 76:1-36.

Bergin, A. E. 1970. The deterioration effect: A reply to Braucht. *J. Abnorm. Psychol.,* 75:300-302.

Bordin, E. 1975. The generalizability of the psychoanalytic concept of the working alliance. Paper presented to annual meeting of the Society for Psychotherapy Research, Boston.

Byrne, D. 1971. *The Attraction Paradigm.* New York: Academic Press.

CURTIS, E. R. 1973. Toward a metapsychology of transference. Paper presented to American Psychoanalytic Association, New York.

FREUD, S. 1913. On beginning the treatment. *Standard Edition of the Complete Psychological Works of Sigmund Freud,* Vol. 22. London: Hogarth Press, 1964. pp. 123-144.

FISKE, D. W., CARTWRIGHT, D. S., and KIRTNER, W. L. 1964. Are psychotherapeutic changes predictable? *Journal of Abnormal and Social Psychology,* 69:418-426.

GREENSPAN, S. and CULLANDER, C. 1975. A systematic metapsychological assessment of the course of an analysis. *J. Am. Psychoanal. Assoc.,* 23:107-138.

HUSTON, T. (ed.) 1974. *Foundations of Interpersonal Attraction.* New York: Academic Press.

LUBORSKY, L. Measuring a pervasive psychic structure in psychotherapy: The core conflictual relationship theme. In N. Freedman (ed.), *Communicative Structures and Psychic Structures.* In press.

LUBORSKY, L., GRAFF, H., PULVER, S., and CURTIS, H. 1973. A clinical-quantitative examination of consensus on the concept of transference. *Arch. Gen. Psychiatry,* 29:69-75. Reprinted in H. Strupp, A. Bergin, P. Lang (eds.), *Psychotherapy and Behavior Change,* an Aldine Annual on Practice and Research. Chicago: Aldine-Atherton, 1973, pp. 512-529.

LUBORSKY, L. and MINTZ, J. *Who Benefits from Psychotherapy, and How?* (The factors influencing the outcome of psychotherapy.) In preparation.

LUBORSKY, L., SINGER, B., and LUBORSKY, LISE. 1975. Comparative studies of psychotherapies: Is it true that "Everybody has won and all must have prizes"? *Arch. Gen. Psychiatry,* 32:995-1008. Briefer version in R. L. Spitzer and D. F. Klein (eds.), *Evaluation of Psychological Therapies.* Baltimore: Johns Hopkins University Press, 1975, pp. 3-21.

ROGERS, C. 1961. *On Becoming a Person.* New York: Houghton-Mifflin.

RYAN, E. R. 1973. The capacity of the patient to enter an elementary therapeutic relationship in the initial psychotherapy interview. Doctoral dissertation, University of Michigan.

STRUPP, H. 1973. *Psychotherapy: Clinical, Research, and Theoretical Issues.* New York: Jason Aronson.

ZETZEL, E. 1958. Therapeutic alliance in analysis of hysteria. In *The Capacity for Emotional Growth,* ch. 11. London: Hogarth Press, pp. 182-196.

APPENDIX A

MANUAL FOR SCORING SIGNS OF HELPING RELATIONSHIPS IN PSYCHOTHERAPY SESSIONS

Read through the sessions and score every example of each of these signs. This manual lists both positive and negative signs. Give a score for each fairly explicit and separable instance (i.e., if the patient says the same thing more than once around the same place, only one score is given—only one score is given for each type of sign). A score includes these components, e.g., HR + 1a5: HR = Helping Relationship; + 1 = positive type 1; a = P says he believes T is helping him; 5 = 5 on a 1-5 scale of intensity.

Positive Type 1	*Negative Type 1*
A helping relationship which depends upon the patient's experiencing the therapist as helpful and supportive to him.	
a. The patient believes the therapist or therapy is helping him (without evidence that his own efforts and abilities have gone into his own change). Example: "I was pleased with the new understanding you gave me in the last session."	a. The patient believes the therapist or therapy is *not* helping him.
b. The patient feels changed since the beginning of treatment in ways he considers to be better. (Evidence is presented that it directly has to do with the therapist's efforts or the treatment.) Example: "I am feeling better recently."	b. The patient feels changed in ways he considers to be worse.

c. The patient feels a rapport with the therapist—he feels understood and accepted. Example: "I feel you understand me."

c. The patient feels absence of rapport—he feels *not* understood and *not* accepted *by the therapist.* (It has to be clear that it is expressed in relation to the therapist.)

d. The patient feels optimism and confidence that the therapist and treatment can help him. Example: "I feel you can help me."

d. The patient feels pessimistic and unsure that the treatment can help him. Patient finds or expects treatment requires things of him he can't do or finds difficult to do.

Positive Type 2

Negative Type 2

A helping relationship based on the sense of working together in a joint struggle against what is impeding the patient. The emphasis is upon shared responsibility for working out the treatment goals, and on the patient's ability to do what the therapist does.

a. The patient experiences himself as working together with the therapist in a joint effort, as part of the same team. Examples: The use of the word "we" in such expressions as "we think" or "we believe." (Try to judge use of "we" which implies an alliance, etc.)

a. The patient experiences himself as not working together with the therapist. . . .

b. The patient shares similar conceptions about the etiology of his problems. In order to score this it is necessary to know the therapist's conceptions.

b. The patient has different conceptions about the etiology of his problems.

c. The patient demonstrates qualities which are similar to those of the therapist, especially qualities having to do with tools for understanding. Example: "I feel I can analyze myself now much as we have done here." (This last sign begins to show the development of a capacity to do himself autonomously and without the therapist what they did together.)

c. The patient sees himself as *not* having the tools for understanding himself.

APPENDIX B

MANUAL FOR SCORING THERAPISTS' BEHAVIORS WHICH FACILITATE OR INHIBIT THE DEVELOPMENT OF HELPING RELATIONSHIPS

Introduction

These items are the counterpart of the Helping Relationships Manual (Appendix A)—they are the therapist's behaviors which facilitate or inhibit the helping relationship. Every instance is to be coded with the item number in the manual. A score includes these components, e.g.: THR + 1a5: THR = Therapist's Helping Relationship; + 1 = positive Type 1; a = therapist believes he is helping patient; 5 = a rating on 1-5 scale of intensity.

Positive Type 1
Giving help behaviors

a. The therapist believes he is helping the patient and conveys a sense of wanting the patient to achieve the patient's goals.

Negative Type 1

a.

b. The therapist believes the patient has in some way made some progress.

c. The therapist conveys a sense that he feels a rapport with the patient, that he understands and accepts him, and respects him.

b. The therapist believes the patient has *not* made progress.

c. The therapist conveys a sense of *lack* of rapport, understanding, acceptance and respect. *Example*: "I do not under-you." (In a general sense, not just informational.) (Behaviors in which the patient is put down by jokes at the patient's expense or other such behavior.)

Positive Type 2
Facilitating "we" behaviors

Negative Type 2

a. The therapist says things which show that he feels a "we" bond with the patient, that he feels a sense of alliance with the patient in the joint struggle against what is impeding the patient. (Just scoring all "we's" is insufficient; the usage must convey presence of a bond or team, etc.)

a.

b. The therapist conveys that he accepts the patient's growing sense of being able to do what he (the therapist) does in terms of using the basic tools of the treatment. The therapist can accept the fact that the patient also can reflect on what the patient is saying and come up with valid observations.

b.

c. The therapist refers to experiences that he and the patient have been through together, building up, as it were, a joint backlog of common experiences. (Score here any such references by the therapist to some past event they have been through together in the treatment.)

c.

GLOBAL RATING SCALES FOR HELPING RELATIONSHIPS

These ratings are to be done at the end of *each* session, just after scoring the Helping Relationship Manual.

1. Patient: Type 1: Patient feels the therapist is helping him

1	2	3	4	5	Brief description of behaviors on which rating was based:
Very much Negative	Some Negative	Middle	Some Positive	Very much Positive	

2. Patient: Type 2: Patient feels he is working with the therapist and will be able to use the tools himself

1	2	3	4	5	Brief description of behaviors on which rating was based:
Very much Negative	Some Negative	Middle	Some Positive	Very much Positive	

3. Therapist behaviors facilitating or inhibiting a Helping Relationship Type 1

1	2	3	4	5	Brief description of behaviors on which rating was based:
Very much Negative	Some Negative	Middle	Some Positive	Very much Positive	

4. Therapist behaviors facilitating or inhibiting a Helping Relationship Type 2

1	2	3	4	5	Brief description of behaviors on which rating was based:
Very much Negative	Some Negative	Middle	Some Positive	Very much Positive	

Part III

INTERPERSONAL INFLUENCES ON PERSONALITY CHANGE

7

The Psychotherapeutic Technique of "Reframing"

PAUL WATZLAWICK, PH.D.

According to an old *bon mot,* an optimist is a man who says of a bottle that it is half full while a pessimist complains that it is half empty—and yet, both mean the same bottle and the same quantity of wine. The difference involved here is based on their different views of the same reality, but it should be at once clear that neither view is more "correct," "saner" or more "reality-adapted" than the other. Similarly, when Alexander the Great simply cut through the knot by which Gordius, the King of Phrygia, had tied the yoke to the shaft of his chariot, he obviously acted on a different view of the problem: how to separate the cart from the yoke, not how to untie the Gordian knot (which many people before him had tried unsuccessfully). And five centuries later the Greek stoic philosopher Epictetus made his famous statement: "It is not the things themselves that trouble us, but the opinions we have about the things."

While most workers in our field will agree that a person's "reality adaptation" is the most important criterion of his sanity or insanity, few bear in mind that when talking about reality we are likely to confuse two very separate orders of reality: one that deals with the physical properties of the objects of our perception, and a second-order reality based on the attribution of *meaning* and of *value* to these objects (Watzlawick, 1976). This, obviously, is what Epictetus meant.

Although it is undoubtedly true that in the case of a particularly

119

severe dysfunction the disturbance may eventually invade a person's first-order reality in the guise of delusions, hallucinations, etc., we find that the overwhelming majority of human problems involve only the second-order reality. Within this realm, however, there exist no objective criteria as to what is really real—rather, the meaning and/or value attributed to an object, situation, event, or especially to the nature of a human relationship has nothing to do with supposedly objective, Platonic verities of which sane people are more aware than madmen. If, for instance, a husband defines his view of the nature of the marriage relation by stating, "I know that you despise me," and the wife tearfully retorts, "How will I ever be able to convince you that I love you?", there is no way of establishing objectively who is right and who is wrong, and what the nature of their relationship "really" is. Similarly, a smile is an objectively verifiable event within the realm of our first-order reality. But its second-order reality, that is, the question whether it signifies sympathy or contempt, is beyond all objective verification. Or to return to my starting point: Whether the bottle is seen as half full or half empty has nothing to do with the bottle as such, but with a person's entire frame of reference.

It is my contention that all effective psychotherapy consists of a successful change of this frame of reference or, in other words, of the meaning and value that a person attributes to a particular aspect of reality and which, depending on the nature of this attribution, accounts for his pain and suffering. This may appear a very arbitrary definition of therapy and certainly one that sounds superficial and "unpsychological." But it should be borne in mind that this definition is itself a reframing that creates a different "reality," which in turn makes possible therapeutic interventions that are "impossible" within the frame of other theories of therapy. "It is the theory that decides what we can observe," Einstein told Heisenberg as early as 1926; and in the field of psychotherapy his statement could be paraphrased to read, "It is the theory that decides what we can *do*." To exemplify:

A young, intelligent student finds it increasing difficult to concentrate on his studies. He is very upset by this, not only because he is in danger of failing, but also because he is basically quite interested in his chosen field and believes that there is something very wrong with him for not getting any pleasure out of studying. In addition, he feels guilty for being a financial burden on his parents without having anything to show for their support. Faced with this problem, a therapist can now proceed in one of two very different ways. He can either analyze the young man's resistance to studying, trying to uncover its causes in the past and to lead the student to insight. The other approach to the problem would be to deal with his basic premise, namely that studying should be gratifying and that he should be truly thankful to his parents. This can be achieved by pointing out to him that even under the best of circumstances, studying is an unpleasant chore and that his idea that he should somehow like it is simply unrealistic. The same holds for his feeling of indebtedness toward his parents: Gratitude is one thing; *liking* to have to be grateful is quite another matter. The therapist can then leave it up to him to continue in his unrealistic, immature attitude toward studying, or to have the mature courage of heartily disliking it. He can even instruct him to set aside a brief, limited period every day during which he should ponder all the unpleasant aspects of studying, competing with other students, the anxiety produced by examinations, the irrelevance of many aspects of his studies and their general interference with the more pleasant sides of a student's life. All of this is repeatedly described as a mature, realistic attitude toward life, defined as a mixture of pleasant and unpleasant things. The usual result of this kind of intervention is that the student's performance improves, because his difficulty was not a problem with studying in the first place, but a self-defeating premise *about* studying that has now been successfully reframed.

Another example taken from the same context would be that of a student who claims he cannot study because he is too involved with his extracurricular activities. He realizes that he should devote more time to his books and he tries to force himself to reach a daily minimum of accomplishments, but no matter how hard and how long he tries to study, he simply cannot concentrate his wandering mind on his books. In his case an improvement can usually be achieved fairly promptly through a behavior prescription based on the agreement that he would only devote a reasonable but limited time to his study and that at the end of this period, regardless of how much or how little he has achieved until then, he would be free to do anything he wants to do *except* to study. This intervention amounts to a reframing of his second-order reality: Leisure is no longer a most tempting alternative to studying, but has now been turned almost into a punishment (comparable to the predicament of many people who would love to stay in bed on work days, but find themselves wide awake on Saturday and Sunday mornings when they could sleep as long as they wanted). The mirror image of this is the well-known scene in which Tom Sawyer, sentenced to whitewash a long, high fence, manages to reframe his punishment to his friends as a privilege in which they are allowed to participate for a fee.

To the clinician faced with the stark manifestations of psychopathology these examples are bound to seem trivial. They are mentioned here, however, because in their simplicity they show the essence of this type of therapeutic intervention. Reframing, to use a definition given elsewhere, "means to change the conceptual and/or emotional setting or viewpoint in relation to which a situation is experienced and to place it into another frame that fits the 'facts' of the same concrete situation equally well or even better, and thereby changes its entire meaning" (Watzlawick, Weakland, and Fisch, 1974).

This, of course, is no longer psychology but ontology, a discipline that the logician Quine once defined as the theory of What There Is. But what there is, "really" is, is determined by the theory, and thus there are as many (second-order) realities as there are theories. We have already seen that the attribution of meaning and value to an object creates, for the author of this attribution, the second-order reality of this object which in turn then may make him suffer or rejoice. Reframing is thus intimately linked to this never-ending ontological process of creating second-order realities. If successful, it indeed creates for the patient a new (second-order) reality while the first-order reality of his world, the "bare facts," remain unchanged (and usually unchangeable).

This procedure raises eyebrows and serious theoretical objections. Above all, how can such a superficial, manipulative intervention that leaves the underlying problem untouched and disdains insight, have any lasting effect? But this objection is based on the unquestioned assumption that "of course" there is an underlying problem of which the symptom (or equivalent pathological manifestation) is only its surface appearance. What this objection overlooks is that it is itself merely an attribution of meaning (an "opinion" in Epictetus' sense) and by no means a correct reflection of objective reality. The "existence" of an underlying problem is thus not an aspect of the (objective) nature of the human *mind,* but a necessary conclusion to be drawn from the nature of a psychiatric *theory* (in this case from psychodynamics) and the theory determines what can be done and what may not be done. Needless to say, reframing is itself nothing but such a conclusion, drawn from and made possible by a particular theory, that is, the pragmatics of human communication (Watzlawick, Beavin, and Jackson, 1967). Faced as we are, however, with a multitude of often incompatible and sometimes contradictory theories, the only meaningful question to ask is not which theory is more "correct" or reflects reality better than the others, but simply which theory makes possible more effective and rapid results.

This is where the second most frequent objection to reframing arises. How, it is asked, can a person be motivated to accept an interpretation of "reality" that is very different from his own? There are two answers to this question. The first is that successful reframing must be communicated in a "language" that is congenial and therefore acceptable to the patient's way of conceptualizing his world, that is, to his second-order reality. In this connection, mention must be made of the pioneering work of Milton H. Erickson (Haley, 1973) and his concept of "Take what the patient is bringing you." What this amounts to is the necessity for the therapist to learn to communicate with the patient in the latter's own "language," rather than—as is done in the more conventional techniques of therapy—to teach him first a new way of thinking and conceptualizing and to attempt change only after this learning process has taken place. The ability to adopt the patient's view of reality is most imperative in hypnosis, but it is equally useful in general psychotherapy. Within this approach resistance not only ceases to be an obstacle, but becomes the royal road to therapeutic change. This leads on to the second consideration, the use of paradox (therapeutic double-binds) in the service of making reframing acceptable or even compelling to a patient. To exemplify again:

A man in his thirties suffers from great tension during periods of increased sun-spot activity. He carefully consults the available data on solar flares and has found clear evidence of their effects not only on world-wide radio communications but also on his nervous system. He can virtually predict these periods on the basis of rapidly growing nervous tension which eventually makes it impossible for him to go to work and forces him to stay in bed. Friends and relatives have pointed out to him the absurdity of this idea, and intellectually he is inclined to agree with them but cannot, on the other hand, ignore the way he feels. He also mentions that he has had a few abortive attempts at psychotherapy which, if anything, made him feel worse. Under the circumstances, a therapist can again take one of two very different approaches. There is, on the one hand, a large number of possible interventions whose common denominator is that they all, in one way or another, imply that the problem should and can be changed. For this implication the patient is well prepared; he has learned how to defeat it. This does not mean that he defeats it "consciously" or "on purpose" and in bad faith; it simply means that his typical way of reacting to help is to point out that this is not yet the right kind of help, and that his problem is much deeper and requires more and better help. A vicious cycle is thereby established and maintained.

The other approach consists in reframing his problem as having very desirable results: Surely he has noticed how much sympathy and readiness to help his predicament arouses in other people, how willing it makes them to accommodate and exonerate him, how many unpleasant obligations and responsibilities he can thereby avoid, etc. The main thrust of the reframing is thus: Your problem is a good thing, why would you want to change it? For this definition of the reality of his situation the patient is not prepared. He is used to being offered help (which he then rejects as ineffective or inadequate), but not to being told that he should continue doing what he wants to be changed. Above all he is likely to reject the reframing as insinuating a nasty, calculated purpose behind the façade of his distress, but he cannot entirely overlook that this explanation fits the facts at least as well as his sun-spot theory. If the therapist then instructs him to do more of the same, that is, to make full use of these advantages (which the patient cannot permit to be called advantages), a paradoxical situation is created in which the patient is changed if he does and changed if he does not carry out the instruction. For if he continues in his symptomatic behavior, the therapist can praise him for having accepted the reframing and further encourage him to do more of the same, which means that the patient has control over his symptom at least in the sense that he can increase (and by implication therefore also decrease) it; but if he takes the opposite stance and wants to prove to the therapist that his reframing is wrong, he can do so only by decreasing his control over his environment through his helplessness, and this again amounts to a decrease in his symptomatic behavior.

The rejection of a reframing is thus not only no obstacle to, but frequently a desirable precondition for, therapeutic change. Don D. Jackson, the founder and first director of our institute, once treated a couple whose main problem was bitter, symmetrical escalations, interrupted only by short periods of physical and emotional exhaustion. He reframed the situation for them as the result of their unusually deep involvement, for only two people who loved each other very much could fight as intensely as they did. The deliberate inanity of this redefinition of their problem made the spouses determined to prove to him how ridiculously wrong he was. This, however, they could do only by fighting less, just to prove to him that they did not love each other the way he said they did. But as they fought less, they immediately began to feel better.

A mother who describes herself as overprotective greatly exaggerates the importance of the problems that her only son is experiencing during the first few weeks in college. He has never been away from home before and finds it hard to adapt to life in a dormitory, certain aspects of discipline, the noise around him, etc., but is quite willing to muddle through. The mother, on the other hand, believes that he should not be required to put up with all that unpleasantness and should not hesitate to come back home as soon as the situation becomes unbearable for him. It is not difficult to see that she may indeed induce the boy to throw in the towel and to drop out of school whenever the going gets a little rough, and it is equally obvious that by merely pointing out to her what she is doing she is unlikely to stop doing it. However, if in the son's presence it is pointed out to her that breaking away from home is a major achievement in a young man's life, that this achievement is all the greater the more difficult it is and that she should, therefore, make it as tempting as possible for him to return home, the situation is reframed for both of them. Her trying to make life easy for him is now labeled as making it difficult, and making it difficult is defined as an important maternal function, necessary to make him fit for life. Since she is bound to disagree with this, she has no alternative but to "help" him less.

In this volume we are discussing effective psychotherapy. The term is deceptively simple, for what is considered effective change in the frame of one theory may be defined as superficial manipulation (or something worse) in another. Not only the conduct, but also the goal of therapy is determined by the therapist's own second-order reality. Alan Watts once said that life is a game of which rule number one is: This is no game; this is dead serious. And talking about rules, Wittgenstein remarked many years ago that if somebody draws our attention to a particular aspect of a game, it stops being that game. "He taught us a different game in place of our own. But how can the new game have made the old one obsolete? We now see something different and can no longer naively go on playing" (Wittgenstein, 1956). Reframing is a therapeutic technique that utilizes the fact that all "rules," all second-order realities, are relative, that life is what you say it is. For many people this is a bitter pill to swallow. They prefer, in Laing's sense, to play the game of not seeing that they play a game (Laing, 1970), and they refer to their blindness as honesty. For them these remarks were not made and they are urged to forget them as quickly as they can.

REFERENCES

HALEY, J. 1973. *Uncommon Therapy. The Psychiatric Techniques of Milton H. Erickson, M.D.* New York: Norton.

LAING, R. D. 1970. *Knots.* New York: Pantheon Books.

WATZLAWICK, P. 1976. *How Real is Real?* New York: Random House.

WATZLAWICK, P., BEAVIN, J. H., and JACKSON, D. D. 1967. *Pragmatics of Human Communication. A Study of Interactional Patterns, Pathologies and Paradoxes.* New York: Norton.
WATZLAWICK, P., WEAKLAND, J. H., and FISCH, R. 1974. *Change. Principles of Problem Formulation and Problem Resolution.* New York: Norton, pp. 92-109.
WITTGENSTEIN, L. 1956. *Remarks on the Foundations of Mathematics.* Oxford: Blackwell, p. 100.

8

Input and Outcome of Family Therapy in Anorexia Nervosa

BERNICE L. ROSMAN, Ph.D.
SALVADOR MINUCHIN, M.D.
RONALD LIEBMAN, M.D.
and
LESTER BAKER, M.D.

This paper is an account of the development of a family therapy model for the treatment of anorexia nervosa, a behavioral disorder of self-starvation, in children. Although the work to be described has always been characterized by a *family*, in contrast to an *individual*, approach to this illness, the conceptual framework and the strategies of treatment have undergone a differentiation and development of their own. This is the result of our increasing experience with this at one time esoteric but recently more common symptom, and of our efforts to evaluate and reevaluate the effectiveness of psycho-therapeutic techniques. The extent to which we have been successful may be seen in the outcome results which will be presented for 53 cases treated in the past six years.

This work was supported in part by NIMH grant 21336 to Philadelphia Child Guidance Clinic, and NIH grant RR-240 to the Clinical Research Center of Children's Hospital of Philadelphia. The authors wish to thank Sherry Bell and Joyce Kobeyashi for their assistance in carrying out the follow-up study.

Overview

The first published report of the application of *structural family therapy* in anorexia nervosa was published by Minuchin (1970) under the title "The use of an ecological framework in the treatment of a child." In his discussion of the case of a 15-year-old boy who refused to eat, Minuchin contrasted traditional child-psychiatric approaches that localize the psychological disorder within the individual with that of the ecologically minded therapist who is concerned with the child in significant contexts, most typically the family, and whose interventions are directed toward those contexts.

The treatment described in that case exemplifies some of the key aspects of the structural family approach:

1. The therapist focused on the family system, that is, on the family members' characteristic ways of relating to each other, rather than on the individual child. The "crazy" symptom of not eating exhibited by the patient was redefined as an interpersonal problem. Family members were seen as mutually regulating each other's behavior so that changes in any part of the family system affected the functioning of the other parts. While this required a more complex approach by the therapist who had to consider the multiple impact of his interventions, it also offered more opportunities for introducing change.

2. The family system was not conceived merely as a system of interchangeable parts but rather as internally structured (hence the term structural family therapy). Family members have individual characteristics and identities; simultaneously they are members of subsystems within the larger system, that is, spouse subsystem, parental subsystem, sibling subsystem, etc. These subsystems are functionally related in ways that are culturally but also idiosyncratically defined. The structural therapist addresses himself to the dysfunctional relationships within and between the systems. His efforts at changing or "restructuring" dysfunctional patterns in this case were directed toward increasing the unity and executive effectiveness of the parental subsystem, and diminishing a cross-generational coalition of mother and patient against the father. The results would have

been quite different if the interventions had been made because the boy was too close to his mother or was rejected by his father.

3. The therapist focused on the here and now, and essentially worked with the ways in which the family dealt with each other at the present time. Little time was spent on historical reconstruction of the development of the family's problem, the patient's problem, or the "reason" for (the intrapsychic meaning of) the anorexic symptom. Diagnostic efforts were directed toward examining the current dysfunctional patterns of relationships, with particular emphasis on transactional sequences, and the way in which the family organized itself around the illness.

4. Therapeutic interventions consisted of arranging experiences for the family members that would enable them to perceive each other and interact in new ways. This was done by strategic redefining of behaviors (not interpretations of inner thoughts and feelings) and through the assignment of interaction tasks to be done at home. Although this approach is similar in some ways to family behavior modification therapy (Eisler and Hersen, 1973), it differs in that the modifications were planned according to an overall view of the family system and the requirements of restructuring its internal organization.

Many of the points made here briefly have been elaborated elsewhere (Minuchin, 1974) and they are generally applicable to family work with childhood disorder. After this beginning, more cases of anorexia were treated, and a broader research into the familial context of psychosomatic illness in children was begun. In particular, children with psychosomatic asthma and with superlabile or "brittle" diabetes were being treated with family therapy in much the same way as described above (Minuchin et al., 1975). In the course of the study, it was noted with some excitement and interest that although the identified symptoms of the children were all quite different, the family patterns of functioning were similar, with the symptomatic child playing a similar role in the dysfunctional family system. The formulation of a conceptual model of psychosomatic illness in children that outlined specific and treatable characteristics of their family's functioning was a great step forward for us in differentiating our approach to anorexia nervosa.

According to this model of the "psychosomatic family," four general characteristics were identified, and a fifth specified the involvement of the symptomatic child.

First, psychosomatic families were found to be highly enmeshed or overinvolved with each other. Although in all families individual members are regulated by the family system while also functioning in individuaally differentiated ways, in enmeshed families the individual becomes submerged in the system. Interpersonal differentiation is poor, and family members may be seen to intrude into each other's thoughts and feelings to a great extent. It is often hard to tell where one person's business leaves off and the other's begins. Another aspect of enmeshment is the poor differentiation of subsystems. This may result in inadequate performance of functions associated with a given subsystem—for example, ineffective parental control—or in the crossing over of boundaries so that children are inappropriately parental to their parents or siblings. Subsystem boundaries may also be impaired because of the frequent formation of coalitions that occurs in these families as a way of maintaining stability, when a child or children may join one spouse against the other in conflict or decision-making.

Second, these families were found to be very overprotective—not only of the symptomatic child but as a way of family life. Overprotection often extended beyond physical care or concern with illness into other areas of life, and it frequently hampered the development of autonomy and interests or activities outside of the "safe" family.

Third, the families were very resistant to change and denied having any problems other than their sick child. These families are particularly vulnerable to pressure for changes in family organization coming from within, such as a child's reaching adolescence, or from without, such as changes in occupation or geographic relocation.

Fourth, the families had a low tolerance for conflict and inadequate techniques of conflict resolution. In some cases families bickered or complained a lot, while others totally avoided disagreement. However, inability to confront differences to the point of negotiating a resolution was characteristic of all the families. As a result, most of the families lived in a constant state of tension.

Within this type of family context, the symptomatic child was involved in parental conflict in particular ways. Parents unable to deal with each other directly might unite in protective concern for their sick child. A marital conflict might be transformed into a parental conflict over the patient. The child might be recruited by the parents into taking sides or might intrude herself as a mediator or helper. The value of the symptom in regulating the internal stability of the family seemed to reinforce both the continuation of the symptom and the peculiar aspects of the family organization in which it emerged.

The development of this conceptual framework greatly facilitated the therapists' work with the anorectic patients and their families. Each family had its own particular style of interaction, its own set of conflictual issues and stresses to which it was responding; nevertheless, awareness of the underlying similarities in family organization enabled the therapists to zero in more quickly on the problems and to develop a systematic program of therapy. An outline of this program, its goals, and overall strategy will not do justice to the many ingenious interventions and family tasks devised by the therapists to accommodate the individual styles and needs of the families. Some of these have been described elsewhere (Minuchin, 1974, chapter 12; Liebman, Minuchin, and Baker, 1974 a and b; Combrinck-Graham, 1974; Rosman, Minuchin, and Liebman, 1975) and other descriptions will follow in later publications. We believe, however, that the overall effectiveness of the treatment, carried out to date by 16 different therapists, comes from the development of a general strategy based on this conceptual schema.

The first step in treating this illness is to eliminate the symptom of not eating. This may seem to be a rather paradoxical statement, because after all, everybody, using any form of treatment, wants or expects to cure the symptom. Usually, however, this is considered to be the ultimate goal, with earlier stages of treatment devoted to uncovering causes, or resolving conflicts, or rewarding improved behavior and so forth. It is our view, however, that although the underlying problems may take a while to clear up, the symptom must be dealt with at the beginning. Anorexia is a destructive and potentially fatal illness. The therapist must reverse this process as rapidly as possible. The emotional charge of this behavior keeps the family strongly organized around the identified patient and around issues of health and food, thus inhibiting a broader exploration of the family relationships that contribute to the illness. When the symptom is no longer available, submerged conflicts and other dysfunctional patterns that have been circumvented and avoided will emerge to be dealt with in treatment.

A variety of strategies are employed to accomplish symptom remission. Slightly more than half of our patients were admitted to a pediatric medical unit for a brief period of from one to four weeks. This is usually done for medical evaluation, to restore some of the more physically debilitated patients, and to determine whether a brief period of disengagement from the family scene, coupled with an exposure to a behavioral paradigm in which participation in activities is made contingent on weight gain, will reverse the eating behavior. Other patients were treated completely on an outpatient basis. Family therapy begins in almost all cases with a session in which the therapist meets with the patient and family around the lunch table. This practice derives from the ecological schema mentioned earlier according to which the wise therapist looks at the problem in its context. The ensuing family encounters at the lunch sessions are programmed by the therapist in a variety of ways (Rosman, Minuchin, and Liebman, 1975) so as to accomplish three goals:

1. To change the family's perceptions of the patient as a helpless, sick, or crazy person and to broaden the therapeutic focus to include the rest of the family. This relieves the patient of the need to carry the burden for the others.

2. To redefine the eating problem as an interpersonal problem. This permits changing the arena of conflict so that the battle may be carried on more directly with less harm to the patient.

3. To block the parents from using their child's deviant behavior for detouring conflict. The motive force for the maintenance of the symptom will thus be removed.

Changes in the family organization which have been initiated in the therapy sessions are reinforced by family interaction tasks to be done at home. When these interventions are successful, and we have some good evidence that they usually are, a rather rapid remission of the symptom will be achieved.

The therapist who from the first has had to deal with overprotectiveness, enmeshment, rigidity, and poor conflict resolution around the eating issue now moves into other areas of life where these patterns are pervasive. As the symptoms of anorexia diminish, other family problems emerge, sometimes revealed in the most trivial events of daily life which can then be explored in the therapy. For example, the six members of one family all had the same socks which were washed together, causing unresolvable arguments about which socks belonged to whom. The opening and shutting of doors and the maintenance of privacy (Aponte and Hoffman, 1973), the distribution of responsibility for household chores, conflicts over discipline, all provide content for the therapist to deal with in his work with the family. The goals for this middle period of therapy are clarification of boundaries, developing problem- and conflict-solving strategies, and increasing the life space of family members. This can be achieved only if the family and parents are less preoccupied with the medical problems of the patient.

In the final stage of treatment, when the eating problems are more remote and family members are functioning at a more differentiated level, the therapist is able to deal with some of the specific and more long-standing problems coming from within the subsystems. Marital problems of the spouses, sibling and peer relations of the children can be treated in separate sessions when required. It is very important to deal with these issues in order to avoid a recurrence of the illness or of other symptoms in the patient or in other family members, and to enhance the individual development of family members.

Within this overview of the structural family approach to anorexia nervosa, we must go to one further level of differentiation. On the basis of a survey of the work of the 16 therapists with all of the 53 patients, it seems that the general schema applies to the treatment of all the families, but that specific goals of family restructuring vary systematically with the age of the child and the developmental stage of the family. The therapists have been sensitive to these differences and have modified the treatment accordingly.

Preadolescents

First let us consider the youngest group, the preadolescents ranging in age from 9 to 12. Fourteen of the patients, or 25 percent, were in this age range. For these families, therapists almost universally stated as their primary goal *"increasing parental effectiveness,* parental control, strengthening the parental coalition especially around executive functioning." To begin this process, some of the parents in the lunch sessions were encouraged to work together to force their child to eat, particularly when the child was most defiant and resistant. Other parents were instructed to maintain a behavioral paradigm at home, similar to that used at the hospital. Parents were helped to become effective at controlling their children's behavior and in setting limits. This strategy not only served to diminish the symptom but reinforced the boundaries between subsystems, increased the distance between parents and child, and minimized the child's involvement in parental conflict. Although these tactics seemed to reduce the autonomy of the patient, the reverse actually proved to be the case. The child, while anorectic, had been trapped in the conflict with and between the parents. Freed from this position, the child was able to return to the normal tasks of developing competencies at home, in school, and in social life which had been neglected during the illness. Positive effects of this strategy on the patient could be seen, not only in symptom remission, but in a more relaxed and cheerful affect state, the giving up of babyish behaviors, and better relations with siblings. When working with this age group, therapists used family sessions initially, shifting to parent-only sessions in the later phases. The preadolescent patients were not seen individually.

Adolescents

The adolescent group was the most numerous in the sample treated; 31 patients, or 60 percent, were between 13 and 16 years of age when first seen. Therapists' aspirations for children in this age group were directed toward *developing autonomy and increasing independence.* Parents and children in some cases were disengaged around the issue of eating and redirected toward negotiating more typical adolescent conflicts associated with this developmental period.

In other cases, children were encouraged to become more self-sufficient in monitoring their own diets, but with the parents supervising the weight gain and behavioral regime. Therapists aimed at reducing parental overprotectiveness and fostered increased assignment of responsibilities for the child in the home as well as for the self.

It is interesting to compare our work with this age group to that of Hilde Bruch (1973). This author suggests that the central issue for anorexia nervosa patients is the conflict around autonomy and control. She proposes that an intrusive and domineering early mother-child relationship may result in the patient's failure to develop feelings of mastery and ownership of her own body. The illness is seen as a distorted but heroic effort by the patient to regain control of her body and to assert autonomy. Bruch's therapeutic work is directed toward a more constructive resolution of this problem. Although we agree that our adolescent patients engage in this kind of struggle, we believe that this is only a partial picture. The anorectic patient, while struggling to free herself of the constricting control of the enmeshed family, is herself controlling, manipulating, and intruding into the domains of her parents and siblings, as are all the members of her family with her and with each other. To work with the adolescent patient alone to disengage her from this involvement is to make the therapeutic task more difficult. We believe that only by submitting the mutually restrictive involvement of parents and child to the therapeutic process, clarifying which parts of the struggle belong truly to the patient and which parts belong to others, can autonomy and independence be established. To facilitate this process the therapists push the children into increased peer- and sibling-group participation. In working with adolescents, therapists will see the siblings together and occasionally the individual patient in addition to sessions with the family and the couple.

Late Adolescents and Young Adults

Eight patients, or 15 percent of the sample, were between the ages of 17 and 21. This is the period in which separation from the family is impending or has actually been attempted. Anorexia at this age seemed to reflect inability of patient and family to negotiate a successful launching of the child into an independent life. The therapists worked only initially in family sessions; they moved quickly to separate the patient into individual sessions to foster disengagement and self-confidence, and worked with the parents in marital sessions to reduce their need for and pull on the patient. Subsequently, patients were able to begin or return to college, get a job, rent an apartment, acquire a boyfriend—in short, to succeed in leading an independent life.

We have elaborated these points to emphasize that commitment to a highly structured, programmed approach need not inhibit flexibility in the use of different therapeutic techniques to fit the particular characteristics of the family and the patient. Individual therapy sessions with the patients or the parents in addition to occasional family sessions are most important in the late adolescent and young adult group to underline and reinforce the disengagement and individuation processes which are vital to the successful outcome. Behavioral modification techniques similarly may be incorporated.

Outcome

The characteristics of the 53 patients whose outcomes are reported here are typical for this diagnostic group as described in the psychiatric literature. We have indicated the age range. Patients came from a variety of middle- and upper middle-class backgrounds; all were white. Six of the patients (11 percent of the group) were male. Their cases and course of treatment were similar to those of the girls. Patients were diagnosed as anorectic on the basis of a weight loss of 20 percent or more, not due to any organic cause as determined by the pediatricians. In our sample, the range of weight loss went from 20 to 50 percent, with a median of 30 percent. In their behavior and verbalizations the patients exhibited the pathognomonic signs of anorexia nervosa: denial of hunger, delusional body image, and fear of fatness. Forty percent of the patients had been treated before referral to us, usually with some form of individual treatment; nearly 20 percent had been hospitalized. The interval between onset of anorexia and referral to us ranged from one month to three years; median time was six months; the median course of treatment was six months. These figures do not include three patients who dropped treatment after two or three sessions (attrition of 6 percent).

Therapeutic outcome was evaluated by two criteria: degree of remission of the anorexic symptoms, and a clinical assessment of the patient's psychosocial functioning in relation to home, school, and social adjustment.

Patients were scored as *recovered* from the anorexia when their eating patterns returned to normal and body weight stabilized within normal limits for height and age. If patients improved, that is, gained weight, but still showed some effects of the illness, such as borderline body weight, obesity, problems of eating such as occasional vomiting, etc., a score of *fair* was given. Patients who did not respond to treatment were rated as *unimproved*.

Similarly, in the clinical assessment patient's status was scored as *good* if adjustment in the family situation, as a participant in academic and extracurricular activities at school or work, and involvement with peers were judged to be satisfactory. A rating of *fair* was given when adjustment in one or another of these areas was unsatisfactory. Patients were judged *unimproved* if they were unable to function even at borderline levels and continued to show disturbances of behavior, thought, and affect.

Evaluations were based not only on the patient's condition at termination of therapy but also on information obtained in follow-up contacts with patients, families, and pediatricians. Follow-up intervals ranged from three months to four years, with a median follow-up time of one year, and 25 percent have been followed for at least two years.

Of the 50 patients who continued treatment, 43 made complete recoveries from the anorexia, four were judged to be only in fair condition, three were unimproved and transferred elsewhere for treatment with some success. In the recovered group, two of the children relapsed, were treated again, and have remained in recovered condition for six months or more. If we count only the absolute recoveries, we have achieved 86 percent successful outcome. Since most published samples of this size report success rates more closely approaching a 30 to 40 percent improvement rate on follow-up, we consider our findings to be substantial evidence of effective psychotherapy.

Results of the clinical assessment have been similarly gratifying. Forty-four of the patients were rated as making a good adjustment, three as only fair, and three unimproved. Counting only the satisfactory adjustments, the outcome is 88 percent effective.

It is of some interest that four of the patients returned later for some brief individual counseling. In these cases, the problem or issues did not concern eating but were related appropriately to a later stage of psychosocial development. The purpose of these additional visits was, as one patient so nicely put it, "to work out normal problems."

In conclusion, we have attempted here to review the development and increasing differentiation of a model for effective treatment of a difficult and life-threatening psychosomatic illness. We believe that the increasing specificity of the concepts, and the development of therapeutic strategies closely tied to them, have enabled 16 different therapists to carry out an effective, systematic approach to treatment that is economical and transmissible to other workers in the field.

REFERENCES

APONTE, H. and HOFFMAN, L. 1973. The open door: A structural approach to a family with an anorectic child. *Family Process*, 12 (1):1-44.

BRUCH, H. 1973. *Eating Disorders*. New York: Basic Books.

COMBRINCK-GRAHAM, L. 1974. Structural family therapy in psychosomatic illness; treatment of anorexia nervosa and asthma. *Clin. Pediatr.*, 13 (10):827-833.

EISLER, R. and HERSEN, M. 1973. Behavioral techniques in family-oriented crisis intervention. *Arch. Gen. Psychiatry*, 28:111-116.

LIEBMAN, R., MINUCHIN, S., and BAKER, L. 1974b. An integrated treatment program for ment of anorexia nervosa. *J. Am. Acad. Child Psychiatry*, 13 (2):263-274.

LIEBMAN, R., MINUCHIN, S., BAKER, L. 1974b. An integrated treatment program for anorexia nervosa. *Am. J. Psychiatry*, 131 (4):432-436.

MINUCHIN, S. 1974. *Families and Family Therapy*. Cambridge, Mass.: Harvard University Press.

MINUCHIN, S. 1970. The use of an ecological framework in the treatment of a child. In E. Anthony and C. Koupernik (eds.), *The Child in His Family*. New York: John Wiley & Sons.

MINUCHIN, S., BAKER, L., ROSMAN, B., LIEBMAN, R., MILMAN, L., and TODD, T. 1975. A conceptual model of psychosomatic illness in children: Family organization and family therapy. *Arch. Gen. Psychiatry*, 32:1031-1038.

ROSMAN, B., MINUCHIN, S., and LIEBMAN, R. 1975. Family lunch session: An introduction to family therapy in anorexia nervosa. *Am. J. Orthopsychiatry*, 45 (5):846-853.

9

The New Sex Therapy: An Integration of Behavioral, Psychodynamic, and Interpersonal Approaches

ROBERT N. SOLLOD, Ph.D.

and

HELEN S. KAPLAN, M.D., Ph.D.

The new sex therapy is the brief outpatient treatment of sexual dysfunction in couples by a combination of psychotherapeutic sessions in the therapist's office and behavioral exercises practiced by the couple at home. The method was developed by Dr. Helen Singer Kaplan (Kaplan, 1974, 1975). Formally, it consists of a systematic integration of behavioral and psychodynamic approaches (Sollod, 1975), in addition to a full acknowledgment of interpersonal dyadic factors. This paper will focus on a description of the fundamental characteristics, distinctive features, and rationale of this integrated therapeutic form, as well as its general implication for psychotherapeutic practice and research.

The therapeutic approach described herein differs from that of Masters and Johnson in that it includes explicit acknowledgment of the importance of psychopathology and psychodynamics and relies on a flexible therapeutic strategy rather than on a programmatic, structured format. In the Masters and Johnson approach, for example, the sensate-focus procedure, a mutual pleasuring experience

The constructive criticism of a preliminary draft of this paper by David L. Wolitzky is appreciated.

that involves gentle and sensitive caressing of each partner by the other, is routinely prescribed. The Kaplan method, however, recognizes that some individuals, for example, compensated schizophrenic patients, may find the intimacy of such an exercise quite threatening. Taking the psychopathology of such patients into account may necessitate abbreviating or even bypassing this exercise. In addition, the requirements of a male-female therapeutic team and the restriction on communications between therapists and patients of the opposite sex are replaced by a reliance on the judgment of a therapist who is alert to countertransferential feelings, including possible sexual bias.

At the time that Kaplan was developing her method, there was a progressive change in the composition of the population seeking treatment for sexual dysfunctions similar to that described (Klein et al., 1969) in patients seeking behavioral treatment for phobias. At the beginning, patients seeking treatment had encapsulated, well-defined problems without more general psychopathology. Gradually more people with moderate to severe psychopathology sought behavioral treatment.

The last decade saw the beginning of a more general rapprochement between behavioral and psychoanalytic approaches (Marks and Gelder, 1966; Cahoon, 1968; Marmor, 1971; Wachtel, 1975, 1976), centered largely on the elaboration of theoretical relationships between the two approaches (Wolf, 1966; Woody, 1968). One development has been the growing appreciation of the significance of psychoanalytic concepts to behavior therapy. Feather and Rhoads (1972) discussed this integration particularly as it applies to the treatment of phobias. Silverman (1974), speaking from an analytic viewpoint, recently detailed possible contributions of the analytic approach to nonanalytic therapies. There is a realization that factors relating to learning theory could play a role in analytic therapy (Silverman, 1974; Greenspan, 1975; Wachtel, 1975). The development of sex therapy as a therapeutic form parallels and in many instances antedates a more theoretical integration of behavioral and psychodynamic approaches. As a practical therapeutic form it has developed methods and strategies not always obvious from purely theoretical considerations.

Some aspects of the sexual response make it particularly suitable to a combined therapeutic approach, which explains to a large extent why the integration of behavioral, interpersonal, and dynamic therapies was develop within the context of sex therapy. First, the sexual response in both the male and the female has an autonomic component that is highly susceptible to anxiety. The source of such anxiety (Kaplan, 1974) ranges from superficial concerns with performance to relatively abiding personality traits or deeply rooted conflicts. The voluntary and learned aspects of the sexual response are also important and consist of a differentiated and highly articulated sequence of behaviors, which must be developed in conjunction with satisfactory involuntary responses. In addition, the sexual dysfunction, though discrete enough to be a specific focus of treatment, is replete with meaning to the individual and is an integral part of interpersonal experience. Thus, compared to other symptoms subject to behavioral treatment, a sexual dysfunction is less encapsulated, more global, and usually more related to the whole personality.

Sex therapy exercises, in themselves, parallel less highly differentiated forms of sex, and have been conceptualized by Kaplan as a replacement for the childhood and adolescent sexual experiences which the dysfunctional patient has often missed. From an analytic perspective, these exercises might be viewed as pregenital as they usually do not culminate in intimate genital union, or, in some instances, even in orgasm. Yet it is only through participating in relatively undifferentiated, pregenital sexual activity that both the child and the sex-therapy patient eventually develop the complex behavioral repertoire which eventually becomes integrated in mature, adult sexuality.

BEHAVIORAL, PSYCHODYNAMIC, AND INTERPERSONAL ASPECTS

The sex therapist focuses on the attainment of specific goals through defined behavioral techniques. "The direct treatment of problem behaviors, the deliberate use of social influence, the use of findings from human and animal experiments, training people in the environment, manipulating present environmental events, and an active therapist," all described by Krasner (1971, p. 614) as essential elements of behavior therapy, are present in the new sex therapy. Such behavioral concepts as desensitization, shaping, and reinforcement account to a large extent for the effectiveness of the prescribed sexual exercises. The sensate-focus exercises, for example, may be seen in terms of reinforcing responses incompatible with anxiety as well as shaping more differentiated and appropriate responses. In treating secondary orgastic dysfunction and erectile dysfunction, the exercises combine a gradual approximation of the behavioral goal with relaxation. The concepts of desensitization and shaping apply to the efficacy of these approaches. Likewise, in the treatment of vaginismus there is a behavioral hierarchy as the patient becomes able to tolerate progressively larger objects and then the presence of an erect penis in her vagina. Assertive training plays a part in the approach described here. The direct and open communication of feeling, for example, and ability to make requests of the partners are goals of sensate-focus exercises. Fensterheim (1972) has described a case of sexual dysfunction in which assertive training was the main therapeutic approach. There is also a strong emphasis on the behavior of the partner, who is the main reinforcer for new sexual behavior. Behavioral principles are used as well in some aspects of the therapist's behavior toward the patient. Verbal reinforcement is used generously, particularly to reward a new, desired behavior. If the patient wishes approval from the therapist, such transference is left uninterpreted and unexplored unless it interferes with the attainment of treatment goals.

Even when a behavioral approach predominates, implicit psychodynamic factors play a role in therapeutic progress. The therapist may be seen as a good parent who not only approves of but actually prescribes sexual enjoyment. The therapist often emerges in the patient's dreams, perhaps as a magician who will transform the patient from a child to a fully sexual person. A therapeutic team often arouses the most intense transference, and the therapists' recognition, acceptance, and support of the patient's sexuality may facilitate some resolution of unconscious conflicts related to sexuality. Furthermore, sex therapy, even when pursued on a behavioral level, may result in shifts in the patient's defensive structure as the patient in sex therapy is encouraged to enjoy sexual fantasy, to engage in more varied foreplay, and to accept a wider variety of sexual expression. Previously repressed wishes often become conscious in sex therapy and integrated into a more satisfactory and pleasurable pattern of sexuality.

Psychodynamic concepts also guide the explicit interventions of the therapist according to this approach. Difficulty in a behavioral exercise may be caused by resistance and, after such behavioral interventions as repetition are tried, the therapist explores the nature of the resistance. The therapist may modify the task in light of presumed dynamics, or cognitively restructure the task in order to bypass resistance. At times a more interpretive stance may be helpful. In the stop/start exercise for premature ejaculation, for example, the male lies on his back and his penis is stimulated. For men with conflicts about passivity, such an exercise may provoke anxiety. Using the Kaplan method, the therapist might encourage the patient to take a more active role in initiating the exercise or to satisfy his partner manually or orally after the exercise is completed. Another possibility would be to emphasize the exercise as a means of becoming more masculine by enabling the patient to attain ejaculatory control. Finally, the therapist might provide a limited interpretation of the patient's feelings about the exercise.

Interpersonal therapeutic approaches are another important aspect of the new approach to brief, outpatient sex therapy. The therapist supports areas of strength in the couple's relationship and helps them resolve problems that interfere with the treatment process. Behavioral exercises often bring such interpersonal problems to awareness. The sensate-focus exercise, for example, often is the occasion for one partner to become acutely anxious about possible rejection. Such fears may have an interpersonal basis and the therapist might attempt to resolve them on this level. If there is an impasse on this level— for example, if one partner actually is rejecting and threatening to leave if there is no sexual improvement—the interpersonal level may become the primary focus of treatment. Often the behavioral exercises have a major effect on interpersonal communication as they involve cooperative effort, learning how to ask for attention, affection, or physical stimulation, and learning how to give in a sensitive and responsive way. Growing competence in these areas often strengthens a relationship and facilitates a more general ability to cooperate. The exercises also highlight communication difficulties which may become the focus of therapeutic exploration.

In this approach the relative contribution of behavioral, psychodynamic, and dyadic intervention varies from case to case and depends on the nature and severity of the dysfunction, the psychological makeup of the patient, and the pattern of the relationship as well as the stage of treatment. Some cases may be approached almost completely from a behavioral standpoint; others involve more exploration of feelings, thoughts, motives, and unconscious conflicts, or a focus on the relationship. In such dysfunctions as premature ejaculation or vaginismus in psychologically healthy patients within the matrix of a loving relationship, treatment may proceed rapidly and effectively on a behavioral level. Secondary orgastic dysfunction is often closely related to the nature of the relationship (McGovern, Stewart, and LoPiccolo, 1975), and treatment of the dysfunction thus may involve a focus both on behavioral as well as marital interactions (Snyder, LoPiccolo, and LoPiccolo, 1975). At times, with a neurotic patient, a sex therapy session may resemble that of an individual insight-oriented session in which conflict areas are explored.

In some cases the therapist and the patient choose the degree to which personality change and exploration of unconscious conflicts shall be a part of the therapeutic process. For example, one patient in the initial evaluation indicated that she could have an orgasm only when she was lying on her stomach and was penetrated vaginally from behind. Her original goal was to be able to have an orgasm in other positions. This narrow, behaviorally formulated goal might have been reached by a strictly behavioral approach, but Kaplan explored with the patient the possible goals of increased spontaneity and joy in her sexual life. The patient agreed that she wanted to be more spontaneous and feminine and that having orgasms in different positions was only one aspect of the kind of sexual life she desired. As a result, therapeutic sessions with this patient focused not only on behavioral elements, but also on her thoughts and feelings about emerging sexuality. Dream interpretation was part of the treatment approach, and the patient related dreams that vividly expressed her hidden wishes to remain a little girl and her fear of transformation into a fully sexual woman. In this case the treatment goal was limited to the patient's sexual dysfunction, but the dysfunction defined in a comprehensive enough manner to involve personality change and integration as well as a specified behavioral change.

DISTINGUISHING CHARACTERISTICS

A number of features characterize the therapeutic integration in Kaplan's method of sex therapy: the multiple use of behavioral exercises, the application of such psychoanalytic concepts as resistance and transference to the behavioral exercises, the development of interpretations which, while acknowledging unconscious motivation, are directly related to symptomatic improvement, and the systematic shift in focus from one type of intervention to another.

One aspect of therapeutic integration is the multiple use of sexual exercises. In addition to being viewed as a behavioral technique, the exercises may also be seen as a means of facilitating interpersonal communication and enhancing sensory awareness. In addition, the therapist uses the exercises as a means of continual assessment. Sensate focus, for example, provides a basic structure within which the partners may evidence a wide range of behaviors. The therapist notes the thoughts, feelings, and behaviors of each individual as well as the couple's interaction. What misinterpretation of the exercise occurred, if any? What were areas of cooperation, of disagreement? The therapist explores particularly the anxiety-provoking aspects of the exercise and, if possible, ascertains the origins of anxiety. Viewed in this way, the question of "success" or "failure" of the patient in an exercise is a moot point. The sex-therapy exercise is a clinical *experiment;* no matter what the result, it provides information which can be used to further the treatment process.

The development of therapeutic approaches to facilitate rapid symptomatic improvement is an essential feature of the Kaplan method of sex therapy. At times this process may involve exploration of the significance of such improvement. Anticipated improvement in sexual functioning often arouses deep resistance. Women with primary orgastic dysfunction, for example, may fear that the initial orgasm will bring with it a dissolution of the personality, insanity, or irreversible loss of impulse control. These fears should be addressed and explored by the therapist. To many patients, improvement in sexual functioning itself would not be so threatening were it not for the fear that the entire fabric of the patient's life might change, even in a positive way. Some patients will find that the behavioral exercises can proceed more smoothly when they realize that improvement in sexual functioning is not necessarily accompanied by other major changes in their lives.

One aspect of the new sex therapy is the distinctive nature of the therapeutic relationship. The pattern is similar to that described by Silverman (1974) in a theoretical paper on the integration of psychoanalytic and nonpsychoanalytic therapies. Here, transferential feelings are left supported and uninterpreted if they do not interfere with the treatment process. When they do interfere, the therapist may either modify his or her own stance or interpret the patient's transferential feelings in a limited way. For example, the homework assignments in sex therapy are usually prescribed in a directive manner. Most patients welcome such an approach as their task is difficult enough without their having to decide which exercises to perform. But a patient who has problems in dealing with authority figures may resent the assignment of "homework." If such a patient misconstrues the directions or finds fault with the exercise, the therapist may assume a less directive stance and, in fact, encourage the patient to choose his own exercises from a variety presented by the therapist. If the difficulties continue, the therapist may explore the patient's transferential feelings and offer a limited interpretation, indicating the significance of the patient's distorted view without attributing responsibility in the form of a motive or wish.

The relationship of the patient to the therapist in sex therapy is also distinctive. The therapist is seen as someone who is able, by virtue of experience and knowledge, to assist the patient in gaining competence in an area of functioning that is both difficult and painful. The patient, like the therapist, shifts focus from the exercises themselves to his or her own experience or to aspects of the dyadic relationship. As this is done, the patient realizes that such a shift is provisional and explicitly related to improvement in sexual functioning. Usually, the patient's relationship to the therapist does not change fundamentally during such shifts. The patient's ability to follow a therapeutic contract and, like the therapist, to shift focus from the behavioral to the experiential makes the integration of therapeutic forms possible.

Therapeutic Strategy

The focus of the therapeutic intervention and type of approach shifts continually. The considerations underlying the nature and timing of these shifts as well as clinical sensitivity and practical judgment related to such shifts are essential to the Kaplan approach. A limiting principle of these interventions is that the completion of prescribed sexual experiences and the responses of patient and partner remain the implicit or explicit focus of the therapeutic exploration. The therapist uses behavioral procedures whenever possible and in preference to psychodynamic or interpersonal exploration. Some of the behavioral methods include repetition, bypassing the resistance, or modification of the behavioral exercise in light of presumed dynamics (Kaplan, 1975). If the behavioral approaches are unsuccessful, the focus is shifted more explicitly to dynamic factors. As has been noted, these may relate to aspects of the relationship, transferential feelings, or an unconscious pleasure taboo. Other areas to be explored may include the symbolic meaning of the exercise or deeply ingrained inhibitions.

The sex therapist using this approach thus considers a number of therapeutic levels and relates them to a single line of behavioral exercises. A deft tactician, the therapist relies on precise timing and tactics, and designs exercises that bypass fundamental areas of resistance. One maneuver, for example, is shifting ground before too much resistance develops. A man with both erectile dysfunction and premature ejaculation may experience difficulty obtaining firm erections in the sensate-focus exercise. Instead of continuing the exercise, the therapist may quickly shift to the stop/start exercise for ejaculatory control, moving the focus of attention away from the erectile dysfunction. Therapeutic momentum is crucial; success engenders confidence and further success, whereas initial difficulties may lead to the development of significant resistance and a therapeutic impasse

(Wachtel, 1975). The sex therapist does not overtly explore potential resistance that has not interfered with the behavioral exercises.

Relationship to Individual or Couple Therapy

Although improvement of sexual functioning remains the goal of sex therapy, awareness of individual pathology or difficulties in the couple's relationship often leads to further treatment. When the goals are not reached, individual psychopathology or interpersonal dynamics are usually implicated, and the patient becomes aware that sexual dysfunction is integrally connected with personality or with the nature of the dyadic relationship. Even when treatment is successful, the patient may, in the process of sex therapy, become aware of certain areas of conflict or difficulty and wish to continue in individual treatment. Encouraged by their success in reaching greater sexual fulfillment, the couple may be encouraged to resolve other problem areas in couple therapy. Sex therapy may also be begun concurrently with other therapeutic forms, or after completion of individual psychotherapy. The process of sex therapy may thus facilitate the working through, in the sexual sphere, of changes realized in personality patterns or in the couple's relationship.

RATIONALE OF METHOD

What is the rationale behind the integration of therapeutic approaches in Kaplan's method? The seeming divergences between the traditions are superficial and camouflage a basic unity and common elements. Sandler, Dare, and Holder (1970), for example, pointed out that such psychoanalytic concepts as resistance apply to a wide variety of therapies, including medical treatment. Others see the psychoanalytic situation in terms of behavioral principles. Certainly, many therapies have in common placebo effects, a patient-therapist relationship, and guidelines for the behavior of the patient and of the therapist. Explanations that stress commonalities, however, do not account for the alternation and combination of therapeutic approaches characteristic of sex therapy nor for the fact that insights and approaches of explicitly behavioral, psychodynamic, and interpersonal origin guide specific interventions.

To understand the efficacy of a combined therapeutic approach, the sexual dysfunctions may be conceptualized as self-perpetuating cycles with components at different levels (Wachtel, 1976). The onset of vaginismus, for example, which occurs most frequently in phobic and inhibited women, may be related to unconscious symbolic meaning of penetration. Once vaginismus occurs, however, intercourse itself may be very painful, and for quite conscious reasons the patient will avoid sex. Anticipatory anxiety will reduce the probability of relaxation and pleasure during the sexual act, so there is little opportunity for desensitization. On the interpersonal level, a woman with vaginismus may be attracted to a passive and inhibited male as a result of her personality makeup, her unconscious fears of penetration, as well as her more conscious concern about painful intercourse. Such a male, often sexually insecure, may rely on his partner's continuing dysfunction to insure his sense of security within the relationship or he may develop a complementary pattern of dysfunction. Thus are set up interlocking, self-perpetuating cycles of dysfunction that include unconscious motivations, behavioral aspects, as well as interpersonal components. In addition, the patient's self-concept and self-fulfilling expectations about events in her life include a prediction of continuing dysfunction. Such a person may also have developed a philosophy of life in which duty or suffering to the exclusion of pleasure is emphasized, or she may have friends who are also dysfunctional or sexually nonresponsive.

A therapeutic approach that emphasizes only one element in such a case will not be effective. Psychoanalytic treatment, though it may resolve questions related to the phobic personality style of the patient, will only with great difficulty be translated into behavioral change because the dysfunction will be maintained by continuing physical pain and concomitant anxiety associated with intercourse. The working through of analytic insight and personality change into self-cure of vaginismus would seem to be an inordinately difficult and taxing task—especially without the assistance of a helpful, informed, and understanding partner. Even with basic personality change, one would expect phobic, fearful attitudes and expectations clustered around the sexual dysfunction to continue. The behavioral approach alone would also be ineffective. Although the patient might tolerate larger objects or even her partner's fingers in the vagina, she might become extremely anxious when the penis is introduced—possibly for purely psychodynamic reasons. A positive outcome might also be temporary unless some of the underlying conflicts were resolved. Furthermore, as the patient begins to improve, the partner might attempt to sabotage treatment. The drawbacks of a strictly interpersonal approach to sexual dysfunction are also evident. At times, a sexual dysfunction may be a veiled form of marital dissatisfaction, but more often it involves behavioral and psychodynamic factors as well.

IMPLICATIONS

Sex therapy as it is conceptualized herein exemplifies a comprehensive definition of the therapist's role, quite consistent with Marks' (1971) view that the therapist of the future should have a broad understanding of various therapeutic approaches. In this view, the therapist is flexible enough to focus on a specific problem area that may be significant to the patient and to foster the development of insight and more general personality change. Sex therapy also provides a field for research on different aspects of an integrated therapeutic approach. The relationship of behavioral change to personality change and marital dynamics may be explored. Behavior therapy may lead to significant positive personality changes as indicated by Rorschach responses (Wachtel and Arkin, 1975). There is clinical evidence (Kaplan, 1974) that sex therapy may have, depending on the case, either a salutary or negative impact on individual psychological functioning or on the couple's relationship. Empirical studies related to the question of symptom substitution would be of special interest. The process of therapy may also be studied to define the impact of various approaches as well as the sequence of intervention and change on the behavioral, interpersonal, and dynamic levels of functioning.

The new sex therapy is an area in which clinical experience with integrated behavioral-psychodynamic techniques has accumulated. In this approach, many problems intrinsic to this therapeutic integration have been resolved. Possible extensions of this distinctive therapeutic form or specific aspects of it to other therapeutic problems should be explored. In addition, this specific clinical synthesis of behavioral and psychodynamic approaches can be related to their more general theoretical integration.

REFERENCES

CAHOON, D. D. 1968. Symptom substitution and the behavior therapies: A reappraisal. *Psychol. Bull.*, 69:149-156.

FEATHER, B. W. and RHOADS, J. M. 1972. Psychodynamic behavior therapy: I. Theory and rationale. II. Clinical aspects. *Arch. Gen. Psychiatry*, 26:496-511.

FENSTERHEIM, H. 1972. Assertive methods and marital problems. In R. D. Rubin (ed.), *Advances in Behavior Therapy*. New York: Academic Press, pp. 13-18.

GREENSPAN, S. I. 1975. A consideration of some learning variables in the context of psychoanalytic theory: Toward a psychoanalytic learning perspective. *Psychological Issues*, vol. 9, no. 1. New York: International Universities Press.

KAPLAN, H. S. 1974. *The New Sex Therapy: Active Treatment of Sexual Dysfunctions.* New York: Brunner/Mazel.

KAPLAN, H. S. 1975. *The Illustrated Manual of Sex Therapy.* New York: Quadrangle.

KLEIN, M. H., DITTMAN, A. T., PARLOFF, M. D., and GILL, M. M. 1969. Behavior therapy: Observations and reflections. *J. Consult. Clin. Psychol.* 33:259-266.

KRASNER, L. 1971. The operant approach in behavior therapy. In A. E. Bergin and S. Garfield (eds.), *Handbook of Psychotherapy and Behavior Change.* New York: John Wiley & Sons, pp. 612-652.

MARKS, I. M. 1971. The future of the psychotherapies. *Br. J. Psychiatry*, 118:69-74.

MARKS, I. M. and GELDER, M. G. 1966. Common ground between behavior therapy and psychodynamic methods. *Br. J. Med. Psychol.*, 39:11-24.

MARMOR, J. 1971. Dynamic psychotherapy and behavior therapy. *Arch. Gen. Psychiatry*, 24:22-28.

MASTERS, W. and JOHNSON, V. 1970. *Human Sexual Inadequacy.* Boston: Little, Brown.

McGOVERN, K. B., STEWART, R. C., and LoPICCOLO, J. 1975. Secondary orgasmic dysfunction: I. Analysis and strategies for treatment. *Arch. Sex. Behav.*, 4:265-276.

SANDLER, J., DARE, C., and HOLDER, A. 1970. Basic psychoanalytic concepts: I. The extension of clinical concepts outside the psychoanalytic situation. *Br. J. Psychiatry*, 117:551-554.

SILVERMAN, L. H. 1974. Some psychoanalytic considerations of nonpsychoanalytic therapies: On the possibility of integrating treatment approaches and related issues. *Psychotherapy: Theory, Research, and Practice*, 11:298-305.

SNYDER, A., LoPICCOLO, L., and LoPICCOLO, J. 1975. Secondary orgasmic dysfunction: II. Case study. *Arch. Sex. Behav.*, 4:277-284.

SOLLOD, R. N. 1975. Behavioral and psychodynamic dimensions of the new sex therapy. *Journal of Sex and Marital Therapy*, 1:335-340.

WACHTEL, P. L. 1975. Behavior therapy and the facilitation of psychoanalytic exploration. *Psychotherapy: Theory, Research, and Practice*, 12:68-72.

WACHTEL, P. L. 1976. Interaction cycles, unconscious processes, and the person-situation issue. In N. Endler and D. Magnusson (eds.), *Interactional Psychology and Personality*. New York: Wiley.

WACHTEL, P. L. and ARKIN, A. 1975. Projective test assessment before and after behavior therapy. City University, New York. Unpublished manuscript.

WOLF, E. 1966. Learning theory and psychoanalysis. *Br. J. Med. Psychol.*, 39:1-10.

WOODY, R. H. 1968. Toward a rationale for psychobehavioral therapy. *Arch. Gen. Psychiatry*, 19:197-204.

Part IV

SOCIAL FORCES AND PERSONALITY CHANGE

10

Patient Attitudes Toward Sex of Therapist: Implications for Psychotherapy

VIRGINIA DAVIDSON, M.D.

In the last 25 years the claim has often been made that women physicians and therapists* are less preferred by the public, and therefore by patients, than men (Williams, 1946; de Beauvoir, 1971; Chesler, 1971; Rice and Rice, 1973; Jackson, 1973; Engleman, 1974; Fabrikant, 1974; *Report of the Task Force on Sex Bias and Sex-Role Stereotyping in Psychotherapeutic Practice*, 1975). Evidence for this claim ranges from the personal experiences of women to survey research involving the public at large or populations of patients. Two studies examine the public's acceptance of women physicians (Williams, 1946; Engleman, 1974); although 28 years separate their publications, both found that male physicians were preferred. This result suggests that, despite the social changes in women's roles and status in our society during those elapsed years, there has probably been little change in the general public's acceptance of women in traditionally male occupations. The more recent study indicates that, of all women physicians, psychiatrists are most accepted by the public;

The author is indebted to Chandler Davidson, Ph.D., and to Chad Gordon, Ph.D., for their assistance in preparation of various statistical portions of the study, and to Chandler Davidson, Ph.D., and Robert Roessler, M.D., for their encouragement in the early phases of the project.

* In this paper, physician and therapist will be used interchangeably, unless otherwise noted. Therapist, however, refers to someone with Ph.D.-level training if a nonmedical person.

this finding suggests that information about preference for physicians by sex cannot be extrapolated to include psychiatrists, and vice versa. The available survey data on this subject are so scant, however, that the categories physician and psychiatrist will not always be sharply distinguished in this paper.

Excepting the present study, one survey of psychiatric patients' preferences for sex of therapist has been carried out (Chesler, 1971). Most of the recent claims that patients prefer male therapists can be traced to this work, which will be reexamined and discussed with the present findings.

The psychotherapeutic research literature reflects little interest in the variable of sex, of patient or therapist, as it relates to the process or outcome of therapy. The index of Bergin and Garfield's *Handbook of Psychotherapy and Behavior Change* (1971) contains no entries related to sex under "patient" (19 entries) or "therapist" (35 entries). However one interesting study discussed in the text (Wyrick and Mitchell, 1969) describes significant differences between female patients' perceptions of female therapists' effectiveness and empathy. One discovers, however, that the "patients" in this investigation are one male and one female actor who *pretend* to need advice from a college counselor who, in turn, pretends to be a therapist. Another example is a study by Simon (1973), who reports that patients prefer male therapists; the "patients" are psychology undergraduates pretending to be in need of psychological counseling. So it goes—one is reduced to discussing make-believe situations to discover the research done on this topic. I mention these studies to underscore the paucity of available research in this area; it is impressive that investigations of this nature, which strongly suggest differential responses between the sexes of patients and therapists, have not been applied to the research of the *real* patient-therapist relationship.

WHAT IS THE RELATIONSHIP BETWEEN SEX OF PATIENT, SEX OF THERAPIST, AND THE PROCESS AND OUTCOME OF THERAPY?

This question emerges from time to time, often in the writings of women therapists. Based on a survey of men and women psychiatrists, Evelyn Ivey (1960) noted that women psychiatrists were more likely than men to consider the sex of the psychiatrist a significant factor in the treatment of patients. She observed further:

> Although psychiatric literature abounds with descriptions of treatment techniques, the importance of the interpersonal relationship between the doctor and the patient and the countertransference and transference problem, few authors related these to the sex of the therapist or specifically referred to his (sic) sex (p. 622).

This observation seems as applicable today as it was in 1960. There are indications, though, that this situation may be changing, largely as a result of the women's movement and the particular emphasis given to women's therapy by women professionals in psychiatry, psychology, and social work (Stevens, 1971; Chesler, 1972; Ash, 1974). Consciousness-raising has reached even the traditionally conservative world of the woman psychiatrist (Kirkpatrick, 1975), and is increasingly considered as a therapeutic modality for some women patients (Brodsky, 1973; Kirsch, 1974). Women professionals are investigating their minority-group status within the professions and are questioning how this status affects their training and job functioning. Wolman and Frank (1975) observed professional women in predominantly male group settings; the jarring results of this study show that the women became group deviants, isolates, or low-status members as a price of membership. This process occurred independently of the personality characteristics of the individual women, who responded to the situation with depression.

It seems no longer possible to deny that the sexes of the patient and the therapist are salient variables in the therapeutic relationship, and that careful investigation of this subject, with all the attendant ramifications for psychotherapy, has yet to be done. Many current feminist writings about psychotherapy and women are dismissed by serious researchers because of the apparent extravagance of their claims; yet to these writers we owe our increased awareness of the importance of investigating the issues concerning women and mental health.

Orlinsky and Howard (in press) demonstrated their interest in these issues with their decision to reevaluate data obtained in 1964.

The authors note that *at that time* they considered the fact that all their patients and some of their therapists were women to be insignificant. They take seriously the feminists' allegations that male therapists may not be able to understand the problems of today's women patients, and ask whether some women do better in therapy with male or female therapists. A reanalysis of their data shows that single, depressed women patients respond differently to male and female therapists; they conclude that such women patients feel more support and satisfaction from treatment with a woman therapist. To my knowledge, this is the only study which attempts to relate sex to therapist, sex to patient, and diagnosis to therapeutic outcome, although Van Atta et al. (1974) note that depressed males and depressed females elicit different responses from therapists in terms of activity, and question what effect therapist response to female sexuality has on the encounter.

No studies on the effectiveness of women therapists compared with men have been conducted. The only data on that subject are indirect, and derive from Margaret Rioch's successful experiment (1963) in retraining college-educated housewives as counselors. Since the fantasied ideal of the woman physician-psychiatrist includes infinite capacities for empathy, genuineness and warmth—a "veritable earth mother" (Scher, 1973)—it is even more surprising that no one has investigated whether or not these qualities prevail in women therapists, especially since considerable effort has been expended by some researchers to quantify qualities very similar to those so often attributed to ideal women: empathy, warmth, and genuineness.

WHAT EFFECTS DO PATIENTS' PERCEPTIONS OF THERAPISTS' SEX-ROLES HAVE ON WOMEN THERAPISTS?

The most obvious effect that preference for women therapists or physicians has on women practitioners is an economic one: Women depend on public acceptance for their professional livelihood. Lopate (1968) reports that women physicians are reluctant to discuss sex and sex role differences in medicine; few women have the candor of the woman intern who said: "Denying the differences due to sex is like denying that a patient of yours is going to die." The denial and reluctance extend to supervisors of both sexes who label a woman in training "odd" or "supersensitive" if she is interested in the issues of sex and gender differences in supervision. Since male therapists do not have experiences with patients that incite their curiosity about sex-role differences, only female therapists can bring personal experiences to us for investigation. Imagine the absurdity of a patient's saying to a male psychiatrist, "It certainly is unusual to see a man as a doctor—what do your children think about it?" or "How do you manage to combine a home life with a career?" Yet these remarks are commonly made to women psychiatrists, who must be able to speculate on the importance of such comments without feeling deviant or unusual.

What other factors related to patients' attitudes toward female therapists affect a woman's capacity to be, or to become, an effective psychotherapist? Women therapists function daily in a complex status set. Stevens (1971) notes that "when a woman deviates from these roles (of wife and mother), when she earns 'real money'—she is thought of as filling a man's role." This statement is especially true if she is employed in an occupation that is strongly male sex-typed, such as medicine. Merton describes an occupation as "sex-typed" when a majority of its practitioners belong to one sex, and when there is an associated normative expectation that it should be this way (Epstein, 1970). Epstein notes that the sex status of the person in the minority sex becomes as, if not more, important as the occupational role.

The woman doctor or lawyer evokes a set of ambiguous responses from her surroundings; observers may be more interested in her sex than in her job performance. This heightened interest in the sex of the woman therapist is often related to her minority status, and may explain much of her patients' behavior. It may also explain why female practitioners have been more interested than males in exploring the relationship between sex of therapist and interactions with patients. Women therapists encounter continual curiosity and perplexity from both men and women patients regarding their roles as physicians. Questions concerning marital status and number of children are quite common. Such comments as, "I've never known a woman who was a psychiatrist!" or "You look much too young to have been to medical school!" or "I thought all psychiatrists smoked pipes and had beards!" occur in one context or another with almost every new patient. Benedek (1973) aptly noted the importance of responding to requests for certain kinds of factual information, regardless of the patients' motives. She felt that these exchanges occurred between patient and therapist *only because the therapist was a woman.* I would agree, and add that these exchanges constitute a part of the ambiguity women experience when they function in the complex status-set described earlier.

Do Patients Prefer Male Therapists?

A study by Chesler (1971) has been cited as evidence for the claim that most male and female psychotherapy patients prefer male therapists, but the data in her study do not bear out this contention. The analysis is based on interviews with 1001 middle-income clinic outpatients who sought therapy in New York City from 1965 to 1969. Respondents were not asked about their preference for sex of therapist, however, and only about one quarter (258) voluntarily expressed a preference or voiced no preference. There is no indication, unfortunately, that this self-selected subsample is representative of the larger one. Assuming that it is representative, Chesler's data still do not bear out the claim that most patients of either sex prefer a male therapist. Her findings on this point are shown in Table 1.

Table 1

Patients' Preference for Sex of Therapist

Therapist Preference	% Male respondents (N = 159)	% Female respondents (N = 99)	% Total (N = 258)
Male	49	40	45
Female	31	25	29
No preference	20	35	26

Source: Chesler (1971)

While the modal choice—for both sexes of respondents—is a male therapist, a majority expressed no preference or preference for a woman therapist. It is true, obviously, that more respondents who did voice a preference chose the male therapist. But this reading of the data differs from the claim that most patients *prefer* a male therapist.

Eldred and Washington's study (1975) of 158 outpatient heroin addicts, which included questions to patients about preferences for sex of therapist, revealed that the majority had no preference (86 percent of the men and 72 percent of the women) and those with a preference were about equally divided on their endorsement of the two choices.

The present study was undertaken to determine the attitudes held by applicants for outpatient psychiatric treatment regarding sex of therapist, and preference for therapist by sex. The self-administered questionnaires were given to patients as part of their registration packets, and were filled out in the waiting area. The questionnaire informed patients that the choices they made on the questionnaire would not affect their treatment course in the clinic. They were asked on the questionnaire to indicate preference (or no preference) for ethnicity and sex of therapist. If a preference for sex of therapist was indicated, a checklist of qualities the respondent assumed would be associated with the therapist of the preferred sex was completed.

The Baylor College of Medicine psychiatry clinic is a middle-income clinic, geared mainly, but not exclusively, to psychotherapy. Fees range from approximately 10 to 35 dollars per session, client incomes from $6,000 to $23,000 annually. The study was conducted for ten consecutive months in 1973-74; demography of the subject population is presented in Table 2.

The sample contained a relatively diverse population. About two-thirds of the respondents were women. Ages ranged from 14 to 68 years, with a median of 28. White-collar occupations predominated, although the blue-collar work force was represented as well. Years of schooling ranged from 5 to 19, with slightly more than half of the subjects having at least some college education. By religion, Protestants predominated (56 percent), followed by Catholics (23 percent). The overwhelming majority were "Anglos," although blacks, Mexican-Americans, and other ethnic groups were included. The findings regarding sex preference for therapist indicate that 50 percent of the sample expressed no preference for sex of therapist, 35

TABLE 2

Demographic Characteristics

	Percentage	Number
Total	100	272
Sex		
Women	65	178
Men	35	94
Age		
14-27	52	140
28-68	50	132
Occupation		
Student	15	39
Blue-collar	11	30
White-collar	54	143
Housewife	17	44
Retired	0	1
Unemployed	3	9
Years of education		
5-12	43	116
13-19	57	151
Religious preference		
Catholic	23	62
Protestant	56	149
Jewish	3	9
Other	6	15
Agnostic/atheist	12	33
Marital status		
Married	44	120
Single	27	73
Widowed	1	2
Separated	11	29
Divorced	17	48
Ethnicity		
Anglo	83	220
Black	7	19
Mexican-American	3	8
Other	7	18
Preference for ethnicity of therapist		
Anglo	30	81
Black	1	3
Mexican-American	2	4
Other	2	4
No preference	65	172
Preference for sex of therapist		
Male	35	95
Female	15	40
No preference	50	134

percent preferred male therapists, and 15 percent preferred female therapists. This compares with Chesler's finding (1971) of 26 percent expressing no preference, 45 percent preferring male therapists, and 29 percent preferring female therapists. It is obvious that the modal choice has shifted in these two studies from that for a male in Chesler's sample to that of no preference in the present study. Whether this difference can be attributed to demographic variations in the two samples, regional differences, or shifts in attitude over time, cannot be said. In both studies, however, among both male and female respondents who express preference, a male therapist is preferred.

One of the most interesting observations about these data is that there are generally no large differences in preferences for sex therapist among or within the various demographic categories; little differ-

TABLE 3

Preference for Sex of Therapist by Selected Characteristics
of Respondents

Respondents' Characteristics	Number	% Prefer male therapist	% Prefer female therapist	% No preference
Male	93	34	14	52
Female	176	36	15	49
* 14-27 yrs	139	28	19	53
* 28-68 yrs	130	42	11	47
Blue-collar	28	47	14	39
White-collar	142	55	6	39
No college	113	34	15	51
Some college	152	36	15	49
Catholic	61	39	10	51
Protestant	147	33	13	54
Other[1]	57	35	26	39
Married	119	30	15	55
Single	72	35	18	47
W/S/D[2]	78	44	11	45
Anglo	219	37	14	49
Other[3]	44	27	16	57

1 other = Jewish, agnostic/atheist, and "other"
2 W/S/D = widowed, single, and divorced
3 other = black, Mexican-American, and other
* significant at 0.05 level.

ence exists between males and females, white- and blue-collar groups, college and no-college groups, and Catholics and Protestants. The two exceptions to this observation are marital status and age (Table 3).

For age of respondent, we note that with increasing age there is an increasing tendency to prefer male therapists; this relationship holds when sex of respondent is controlled (Table 4).

TABLE 4

Preference for Sex of Therapist by Age of Respondent
with Sex of Respondent Controlled

	% Prefer male therapist	% Prefer female therapist	% No preference
14-27 years			
Male (44)	30	18	52
Female (95)	28	19	53
28-68 years			
Male (49)	39	10	51
Female (81)	45	11	44

Does this finding mean that attitudes are changing, or does it simply mean that younger persons in any time period are less likely to hold rigid sex-role stereotypes? Without longitudinal data, we cannot say.

The most interesting category is marital status (Table 5). Males in the "widowed-separated-divorced" category have a greater preference for male therapists. Compared with single and married male respondents, the percentage with no preference decreases, and the preference for female therapists increases. Feminists have contended that many women are traditionally drawn to psychotherapy with males for "man-seeking" reasons; perhaps some male patients are drawn to female therapists for similar sex-related reasons.

Female respondents are also more likely to prefer a therapist of the opposite sex when they are in the "single" or "widowed-separated-divorced" category; the pattern is one of the most clear-cut that emerges from the data. If we assume that each of the three categories —married, single, and widowed-separated-divorced—represents a progressively greater degree of estrangement from the opposite sex,

TABLE 5

Preference for Sex of Therapist by Marital Status with Sex of Respondent Controlled

		% Prefer male therapist	% Prefer female therapist	% No preference
Married				
Male	(48)	33	9	58
Female	(71)	28	20	52
Single				
Male	(29)	31	17	52
Female	(43)	37	19	44
Wid-Sep-Div				
Male	(16)	44	25	31
Female	(62)	44	8	48

TABLE 6

Reasons for Preferring a Therapist of a Particular Sex* (Given only by respondents who expressed a preference)

	Reasons for preferring: male therapist (N = 95) %	Reasons for preferring: female therapist (N = 40) %
1. I would feel more comfortable in a man's/woman's presence	70	65
2. He/she would be more attractive to me personally	17	23
3. I could talk more freely about my problems	61	70
** 4. He/she would understand my problems better	30	68
5. He/she would probably be very intelligent	7	20
** 6. Past experience with male/female doctors has been satisfactory	48	28
** 7. I prefer male/female doctors in general	44	18
8. Past experience with female/male doctors has been unsatisfactory	12	23
9. Other	16	15

* Percentages add up to more than 100 because multiple choices of reasons were allowed.
** Significant at 0.05 level.

the findings suggest a link between estrangement and therapist preference that deserves further investigation.

Looking at the reasons most frequently checked for preference of
sex (Table 6), we see that "feeling comfortable" is the most popular
item for both male and female respondents. Being able to "talk
freely" is second, and there are no other choices which are checked
by more than 50 percent of respondents of both sexes. Intelligence
of therapists is a relatively unpopular item, checked more often for
female than male therapists. This is surprising in view of other
findings, which suggest that women physicians are seen as less competent than men.

TABLE 7

Reasons for Preferring a Therapist of a Particular Sex with Sex of Respondent Controlled

| | Reasons for preferring: | | | |
| | male therapist | | female therapist | |
	Males (N = 32)	Females (N = 63)	Males (N = 13)	Females (N = 27)
1. Comfortable	69	70	62	67
2. Attractive	6	22	62	4*
3. Talk freely	72	56	46	82
4. Understand	38	25	54	74
5. Intelligent	3	10	46	7**
6. Past MD good	44	51	31	26
7. Prefer in general	34	49	31	11
8. Past MD bad	9	13	31	19
9. Other	13	18	39	4**

* Significant at 0.001 level
** Significant at 0.05 level

When these reasons for preference are controlled for sex of respondent, several interesting facts become apparent (Table 7). First,
the category "feeling comfortable" does not change very much, yet
"talking freely" is checked less for women preferring male therapists
than for women preferring female therapists. This suggests that there
are different reasons among women who prefer male therapists than
among those who prefer female therapists. If women are driven by
"man-seeking" behavior, it would seem that the category "attractive-
ness" would be checked more frequently. Interestingly, the category
"understanding my problem" is frequently checked by women seek-

ing women therapists. This finding suggests that women who seek female therapists expect better understanding from a therapist of the same sex; women seeking male therapists do not rate "understanding" as an important expected characteristic of the male thera pist. Persons of both sexes expect to be able to "talk more freely" with a therapist of the same sex.

The major findings of this study can be summarized as follows:

1. Half of the respondents had no preference for sex of therapist. Among the remainder, a male therapist was preferred by a ratio of about 2:1. This distribution held when sex of respondent was controlled.

2. Young patients were more likely to express no preference for sex of therapist and to be the group most likely to prefer female therapists.

3. Marital status was the category that showed the most striking variation in preference for sex of therapist. This finding suggests that patients in the different marital categories may have differing therapeutic needs—or, at any rate, might be expected to have the strongest response to the sex of the therapist.

4. Patients who prefer male therapists have somewhat different reasons for their preference than patients who prefer female therapists. This suggests that female therapists are perceived by patients as possessing different personality characteristics than male therapists, at least by those patients who seek female therapists.

The relationship of sex and sex-role behavior of both patients and therapists has yet to be carefully investigated with regard to the process and outcome of psychotherapy. The women's movement has so dramatically called our attention to the importance of these issues that only the most obtuse clinician can continue to ignore their importance for patient and therapist alike. Women patients, in particular, has become more sensitive regarding the attitudes their therapists (and their physicians in general) hold toward them. This heightened sensitivity exists partly because of studies such as the Brovermans' (1970), which demonstrated, among other things, that both male and female therapists have stereotypic views of women patients, and that a double standard of mental health exists for the two sexes. Rather than dismiss such studies, it is time to incorporate the questions they raise into our research.

The psychotherapy literature does not reflect the existence of two sexes. More has been written about the galvanic skin response of patient and therapist, the breathing rate of both as an index of anxiety, the eyeblink rate as related to verbal productions, the role of silence, the importance of ambiguity, the effects on the therapeutic participants of filming, recording, or observation, body movement, speech rate, even electromyographic responses than about the variable of sex. Surely it is time for change.

REFERENCES

ASH, M. 1974. The changing attitudes of women: Implications for psychotherapy. *J. Am. Med. Wom. Assoc.*, 29:411-413.

BENEDEK, E. 1973. Training the woman resident to be a psychiatrist. *Am. J. Psychiatry*, 130:1131-1135.

BERGIN, A. and GARFIELD, S. L. (eds.) 1971. *Handbook of Psychotherapy and Behavior Change.* New York: John Wiley & Sons.

BRODSKY, A. M. 1973. The consciousness-raising group as a model for therapy with women. *Psychotherapy: Theory, Research, and Practice*, 10:24-29.

BROVERMAN, I. K., BROVERMAN, D. K., CLARKSON, F. E., ROSENKRANTZ, P. S., and VOGEL, S. R. 1970. Sex-role stereotypes and clinical judgments of mental health. *J. Consult. Clin. Psychol.*, 34:1-7.

CHESLER, P. 1971. Women as psychiatric and psychotherapeutic patients. *Journal of Marriage and the Family*, 33:746-759.

CHESLER, P. 1972. *Women and Madness.* Garden City, N.Y.: Doubleday.

DE BEAUVOIR, S. 1971. *The Second Sex.* New York: Knopf.

ELDRED, C. A. and WASHINGTON, M. N. 1975. Female heroin addicts in a city treatment program: The forgotten minority. *Psychiatry*, 38:75-85.

ENGLEMAN, E. G. 1974. Attitudes toward women physicians. *West. J. Med.*, 120:95-100.

EPSTEIN, C. F. 1970. *Woman's Place.* Berkeley: University of California Press.

FABRIKANT, B. 1974. The psychotherapist and the female patient: Perceptions, misperceptions, and change. In V. Franks and V. Burtle (eds.), *Women in Therapy.* New York: Brunner/Mazel, pp. 83-109.

IVEY, E. P. 1960. Significance of the sex of the psychiatrist. *Arch. Gen. Psychiatry*, 2:622-631.

JACKSON, A. 1973. Problems experienced by female therapists in establishing an alliance. *Psychiatric Annals*, 3:6-9.

KIRKPATRICK, M. J. 1975. A report on a consciousness-raising group for women psychiatrists. *J. Am. Med. Wom. Assoc.*, 30:206-212.

KIRSCH, B. 1974. Consciousness-raising groups as therapy for women. In V. Franks and V. Burtle (eds.), *Women in Therapy.* New York: Brunner/Mazel, pp. 326-354.

LOPATE, C. 1968. *Women in Medicine.* Baltimore: Johns Hopkins University Press.

ORLINSKY, D. E. and HOWARD, K. I. The effects of sex of therapist on the therapeutic experiences of women. *Psychotherapy: Theory, Research, and Practice.* In press.

Report of the Task Force on Sex Bias and Sex-Role Stereotyping in Psychotherapeutic Practice, 1975. American Psychological Association, p. 16.

RICE, J. K. and RICE, D. G. 1973. Implications of the women's liberation movement for psychotherapy. *Am. J. Psychiatry,* 130:191-195.

RIOCH, M. J., ELKES, C., FLINT, A. A., USDANSKY, B. S., NEWMAN, R. G., and SILVER, E. 1963. National Institute of Mental Health pilot study in training mental health counselors. *Am. J. Orthopsychiatry,* 33:678-689.

SCHER, M. 1973. Women psychiatrists in the United States. *Am. J. Psychiatry,* 130: 1118-1122.

SIMON, W. 1973. Age, sex, and title of therapist as determinants of patients' preferences. *J. Psychol.,* 83:145-149.

STEVENS, B. 1971. The psychotherapist and women's liberation. *Social Work,* 11:12-18.

VAN ATTA, R. E., RALPH, K. E., and SCHUBERT, M. A. 1974. Prediction of therapist responses from pre-therapy text variables: A preliminary study. Unpublished manuscript.

WILLIAMS, J. 1946. Patients and prejudice: Lay attitudes toward women physicians. *Am. J. Sociol.,* 51:283-287.

WOLMAN, C. and FRANK, H. 1975. The solo woman in a professional peer group. *Am. J. Orthopsychiatry,* 45:164-171.

WYRICK, T. J. and MITCHELL, K. M. 1969. Relationship between accurate empathy, warmth, and genuineness and perceived resident assistant effectiveness. *Discussion Papers,* Arkansas Rehabilitation Research and Training Center, University of Arkansas, 12. In A. E. Bergin and S. L. Garfield (eds.), 1971, *Handbook of Psychotherapy and Behavior Change.* New York: John Wiley & Sons.

11

Depressed Women: Traditional and Nontraditional Therapies

MYRNA M. WEISSMAN, PH.D.

Considerable attention has been directed recently to the quality of psychiatric care, especially psychotherapy, that women receive (Chesler, 1972). This attention parallels the growth of the feminist movement of the 1970s and is part of a larger reexamination of women's roles and rights. Much of the writing, however, has been in the nature of an exposé (Guttentag, 1975). Nonetheless, the following facts cannot be ignored. Women are by far the largest consumers of outpatient psychotherapy. Most psychiatrists, and therefore most psychotherapists, are men. Psychotherapy as an educational process is influenced by the therapist's theoretical framework and implicit notions about what is normal behavior. Much psychotherapy is based on Freudian concepts, which can include suggestions that women are incomplete and inadequate versions of men and that the appropriate feminine role is one of nurturance, vicarious living, and subordination.

The feminists may argue that the traditional feminine role leads to helplessness, noting that depression, a state of helplessness, is predominantly a female disorder and that traditional therapies en-

This work is funded in part by Grant No. MH26466 from the Clinical Research Branch, National Institute of Mental Health, Rockville, Maryland.

I am indebted to Irene Waskow, Ph.D., and to Barry E. Wolfe, Ph.D., Clinical Research Branch, National Institute of Mental Health (NIMH), for making available the literature on consciousness-raising groups; and to Irene Waskow, Ph.D., to Lenore Radloff, Ph.D., Center for Epidemiologic Studies, NIMH, and to Boris Astrachan, M.D., Yale University, for comments on the manuscript.

courage women to adjust to depressing situations. To correct this situation there has been a burgeoning of informal nontraditional therapies initiated and led by women.

Despite the interest in women's mental health treatment and the increase in alternate therapies, it is almost impossible to draw conclusions as systematic data on these new therapies are unavailable. The situation is confounded by a number of factors: Traditional therapies are diverse (e.g., compare Freudian psychoanalytic therapy with behavior therapy); nontraditional therapies are also diverse (e.g., compare a consciousness-raising group with a self-help career center); there are few systematic data on users, types of efficacy of the nontraditional therapies; * there are no published data on the effectiveness of female as compared to male therapists in traditional therapies. * *

This paper will not be able to shed new light on most of the issues as the data are lacking. A reexamination of the epidemiologic and clinical data that are available, however, can suggest the next phase of study.

This paper has several purposes: to review the data on sex differences in rates and treatment of depressive disorders, which will demonstrate the most common mental health problems and help-seeking of women; to review the evidence based on controlled study for the efficacy of traditional therapies for depression; to describe some of the nontraditional therapies and to speculate on their utility. more prevalent among women than among men. This observation has been confirmed by numerous epidemiologic studies.

THE PSYCHIATRIC DISORDERS OF WOMEN

Alcohol and drug abuse are predominantly male disorders, and schizophrenia shows no clear sex trend. Depression, however, is much

---

* Marcia Guttentag, Ph.D., Harvard University, has recently undertaken a study of women's mental health services that will examine self-help groups. Diane Kravetz, M.S.W., University of Wisconsin, and Morton Lieberman, Ph.D., University of Chicago, are currently surveying women in consciousness-raising groups.

* * D. Orlinsky and K. Howard at University of Chicago and Northwestern University, respectively, have undertaken a reanalysis of data collected on women in outpatient psychotherapy who had been assigned male or female therapists in order to determine the effect of the therapist's sex on outcome.

TABLE 1

Sex Ratios in Depression from Hospital Admissions, Outpatient Clinics and Community Surveys

Source of Data	Place and Time	Disorder	Rates: Females Per 100 Males	Reference
Hospital admissions (state, private, general, and community mental health center)	United States, 1970	All depressive disorders	175	Cannon and Redick, 1970
Outpatient psychiatric services	United States, 1970	All depressive disorders	238	Cannon and Redick, 1970
Community surveys	New York City, 1965	Anxiety and depression	Women have more symptoms	Benfari et al., 1972
	Baltimore, Md., 1968	Depressive symptoms	160	Siassi et al., 1974
	North Florida, 1968	Depressive symptoms	180	Schwab et al., 1973
	Carroll County, Md., 1968	Depression, helplessness	Women have more symptoms	Hogarty and Katz, 1971
	New Haven, Conn., 1967-69	Suicidal feelings	120	Paykel et al., 1974

more prevalent among women than among men. This observation has been confirmed by numerous epidemiologic studies.

Table 1 summarizes these findings for depression. For brevity this review is limited to recent studies and to data from the United States, but the figures are representative. We have recently reviewed the data on sex ratios in psychiatric disorders covering the last 40 years and including countries outside the United States, and have found essentially the same results (Weissman and Klerman, 1976b). Data are available from two sources: clinical observations of patients coming for treatment either as inpatients or as outpatients; and surveys of persons in the community.

Women are More Frequently Diagnosed as Depressed

Studies of patients coming for treatment provide an estimate of illness of moderate to severe intensity as scrutinized and processed by clinical professionals and institutions. Rates of diagnosed disorders are subject to the availability of treatment facilities and the person's willingness to seek and ability to afford treatment.

Hospital admissions usually represent the more severe forms of the illness. In the United States women predominate among hospital admissions for depression. There are approximately 175 women to every 100 men admitted for depressions. The sex difference is much more striking when one looks at the figures for outpatient services where there are 238 women for every 100 men, more than a twofold difference (Table 1).

Are Women More Depressed?

Treated cases do not represent true incidence, since many ill persons do not seek treatment and epidemiologic evidence requires data from community surveys. Such surveys usually include a random sample of persons in a community or a defined nonclinic population. Therefore, information on persons who are both in treatment as well as those who have never received any treatment and would not have been included in the previous figures, can be recorded.

Depressed women still predominate in surveys (Table 1). The sex ratios found in surveys, however, are comparable to ratios found in hospitalized patients but not as high as in outpatient treatment.

The outpatient sex ratio for depression is consistent with patterns of help-seeking and treatment utilization of women in general. For example, the National Ambulatory Medical Care Survey for 1973-74 showed that women outnumbered men 3 to 2 in number of office visits for all illnesses, and women predominate in the use of psychotherapeutic drugs (Parry et al., 1973).

We can conclude that women not only have different mental health problems but different methods of coping with them. These differences are reflected in differing diagnosis and utilization of psychiatric facilities. Women more frequently report depressive symptoms, are diagnosed as depressed, and, in far greater proportion than men, seek outpatient treatment for depression. The ambulatory treatment of depression is, therefore, of particular importance when one reviews the mental health care of women.

How Effective Are the Treatments for Depression?

Treatments for depression on an ambulatory basis can be divided into pharmacotherapy and psychological therapy. Electroconvulsive therapy (ECT) is used for the severe forms of depression in patients when drugs are not indicated for medical reasons or in patients who have not responded to pharmacologic treatments. With rare exception ECT is not an ambulatory treatment and it will not be discussed here.

While this discussion focuses on the efficacy of psychotherapies, it is important to review the evidence for pharmacotherapy since in practice both treatments are employed either separately, alternately, or in combination. Moreover, there has been concern from those involved in women's issues that women may be over-medicated to encourage them to adjust to intolerable situations which, in fact, might require social and political change. Therefore, clarity as to what condition and on what outcomes we can expect the different treatments to be effective may help us to understand their utility. For this discussion acute and maintenance therapy are examined separately.

Antidepressants—Acute Treatment

The discovery in the late 1950s of the monoamine oxidase inhibitors and the tricyclic compounds revolutionized the treatment of depression. These and other antidepressant drugs have been tested in well-designed double-blind, placebo-controlled studies and the results have been well-reviewed (Klerman and Cole, 1965; Klein and Davis, 1969). These results leave little doubt of the efficacy of antidepressant drugs, as compared to placebo, in reducing the acute symptoms of depression over two to four weeks. Acutely depressed patients receiving these medications report improvement in mood, sleep, appetite, sexual functioning, and reduction of suicidal ideation (Haskell, DiMascio, and Prusoff, 1975). Although the drugs do not help some depressed patients and many patients improve with placebo, the accumulated evidence is still strong that drugs, especially the tricyclics, are effective treatments.

Antidepressants—Maintenance Treatment

Maintenance treatment is particularly important since a substantial proportion of depressed patients (40 to 50 percent) experience recurrence and a small portion (10 to 15 percent) become chronic (Weissman and Klerman, 1976a; Robins and Guze, 1972).

Until recently there were no acceptable data on the role of maintenance therapy in preventing relapse. It was unclear how long patients should remain on drugs and how best to prevent a recurrence of symptoms. Over the last three years such evidence has become available.

Table 2 summarizes the results of four maintenance trials of tricyclic antidepressants, all of which involved outpatients. The New Haven-Boston and the Baltimore studies included only women. The Philadelphia study was 80 percent female and the London study 65 percent. In all four studies tricyclic antidepressants prevented relapse and reduced symptoms. Interestingly, the Baltimore study found that diazepam at 12 months was less effective than placebo. The London study found that patients with an incomplete recovery from a depressive episode who continued on maintenance drugs benefited most. The three studies reporting data on social functioning showed either no effect or a minimal effect. The New Haven-Boston study found no difference between amitriptyline, placebo, or no pill on

TABLE 2

Summary of Evidence for the Efficacy of Maintenance
Tricyclic Antidepressants

Place	Length of Maintenance	Drug	Effect of Antidepressants	Reference
New Haven, Ct. Boston, Mass.	8 Months	Amitriptyline/placebo/ no pill	Reduced relapse rate and prevented symptom return. No effect on social adjustment.	Klerman et al., 1974
Baltimore, Md.	16 Months	Imipramine/diazepam/ placebo	Reduced relapse rate and prevented symptom return, improved inter-personal perception.	Covi et al., 1974
Philadelphia, Pa.	12 Weeks	Amitriptyline/placebo	Reduced symptoms at 4 weeks and a trend toward maintaining symptom reduction at 6 to 12 weeks. No effect on participation and performance in family roles or on marital relationships.	Friedman, 1975
London, England	6 Months	Amitriptyline/placebo	Reduced relapse rate. Social adjustment data not reported.	Mindham et al., 1973

the patient's social adjustment. The Philadelphia study found a small effect on participation and performance in family roles, and the Baltimore study noted an effect on the patient's interpersonal perceptions.

In summary, the similarity in findings among studies offers clear recommendation for the outpatient treatment of depression. Maintenance antidepressants are valuable in preventing relapse and symptom return especially if the patient has lingering symptoms following an acute episode. Moreover, there is suggestion that caution should be exerted in substituting the minor tranquilizers for tricyclic antidepressants as maintenance therapy in patients with a definite diagnosis of depression.

Although some recovery of social performance undoubtedly occurs as a result of the reduction of symptoms, medications themselves may have only a limited impact on problems in living, and many investigators have proposed that psychotherapy would be effective in these areas.

Psychotherapy—Acute Treatment

Despite clinical testimony about the value of psychotherapy for acute treatment, we could not find any controlled clinical trials of psychotherapy that specifically studied acute treatment in a homogeneous sample of depressed patients, although some depressed patients have undoubtedly been included in studies testing the efficacy of psychotherapy (Luborsky, Singer, and Luborsky, 1975). There are suggestive pieces of evidence—for example, Auerbach has found that the diagnosis of depression was a positive prognostic sign for a psychotherapeutic effect (Auerbach, Luborsky, and Johnson, 1972).

The Philadelphia study, although designed as a maintenance trial, followed patients during the acute phase when they were assigned to marital therapy versus minimal contact. Marital therapy had a modest positive effect on symptom relief at the end of four weeks (Friedman, 1975). The Baltimore study, also designed as a maintenance trial, showed a group psychotherapy effect on improvement in mood after one week, but this advantage was lost at two weeks (Lipman, Covi, and Smith, 1975).

There are studies under way, however, to correct this gap in data on the acute psychotherapeutic treatment of depression. Rush, Beck, and Kovacs (1975) reported preliminary results from a pilot study in moderately and severely depressed outpatients using twice-a-week cognitive behavior therapy, as compared with imipramine. While the samples are small and results tentative, cognitive behavior therapy was as effective as pharmacotherapy in relieving acute symptoms of depression and resulted in a lower dropout rate.

The New Haven-Boston Collaborative Depression Group has undertaken a 16-week study of the acute treatment of depression using a four-cell design, including individual psychotherapy alone, amitriptyline alone, combined treatment, and no planned treatment. Results will be available in 1976.

Psychotherapy—Maintenance Therapy

Whereas the goal of acute treatment is symptom remission, maintenance therapy is concerned with prevention, health maintenance, and the restoration and enhancement of social functioning. Three of the four maintenance studies described above also included psychological therapies in their designs.

Table 3 shows the results of the maintenance psychotherapies. The New Haven-Boston trial, which used individual psychotherapy given by psychiatric social workers, showed a positive effect for psychotherapy on social and interpersonal functioning, but only in patients who completed the trial without relapsing. This effect was not apparent on symptoms or relapse rate and took six to eight months to develop. Patients who became symptomatic and did not complete the trial showed no benefit from psychotherapy.

The Baltimore study showed a stronger effect for group therapy on areas related to interpersonal functioning, empathy, sensitivity, and hostility, rather than symptom. This effect was evident at 16 weeks, earlier than noted in the New Haven-Boston study.

The Philadelphia study, which was the briefest (12 weeks) and used marital therapy, showed an early effect. The effect was strongest on social functioning and family participation and on attitudes and behavior in marriage. There was also an effect on symptom relief but

Table 3

Summary of Evidence for the Efficacy of Maintenance Psychotherapies

Place	Time	Type of Treatment	Outcome of Treatment	Reference
New Haven-Boston	8 Months	Individual psychotherapy	Improved overall social functioning, performance, communication. Reduced dependency, friction. No effect on relapse rate or symptoms.	Weissman et al., 1974
Baltimore, Md.	16 Weeks	Group therapy	Improved empathetic understanding. Reduced interpersonal sensitivity, hostility and anxiety. No effect on relapse rate or symptoms.	Covi et al., 1974
Philadelphia, Pa.	12 Weeks	Marital therapy	Positive symptom relief but not as great as for drugs. Positive effect on participation and performance of family roles, perception of spouse's attitude and behavior in marriage.	Friedman, 1975

this was not as large as on social adjustment or as shown overall for drugs.

In all three studies the psychological intervention had a positive effect, which was strongest in areas related to problems in living—interpersonal relationships—and less strong or absent in the relief of symptoms of depression per se. The rapidity of the onset of effect suggests that marital therapy may have some additional benefit over the other therapies, but this requires further testing.

Traditional Therapies Do Not Deal With Primary Prevention

The evidence from controlled trials is most encouraging. Several independent studies have shown the efficacy of traditional therapies, both antidepressant drug therapy and psychotherapy, in reducing symptoms of depression, preventing symptom return, and enhancing the social functioning of women after a depressive episode. There is no evidence, however, that these therapies are more than symptomatic treatments or that they will prevent the recurrence of depression once the treatment ends.

Feminists and others have challenged the value of traditional therapies. Since women predominate in the diagnosis, treatment, and reporting of depression, feminists argue that the best primary prevention may be found in reducing the conditions that depress women and in the social retraining of women by other women. This view is exemplified in the writings of Pauline Bart (1975), but other persons, both professional and non-professional, are emerging.

Why Women Get Depressed

There are, of course, many possible explanations for the predominance of depressed women. The finding might be an artifact of women's willingness to acknowledge symptoms and seek treatment, or of men's tendency to deal with depression by alcoholism, drug abuse, or aggression. Alternately, the finding could be real and the result of physiologic, genetic, or social role differences. A review we have just completed on this subject suggests that the predominance of depressed women cannot be fully explained as an artifact (Weissman and Klerman, 1976b). We found no conclusive evidence that genetic and/or endocrine differences between the sexes could account for the predominance of depressed women, and we concluded that at least some of the difference has to do with the role of women.

The *female social-role explanation* asserts that depression in women occurs in greater frequency than in men because women are indeed more helpless. The helplessness is related to real social inequities, as well as learned helplessness, which is part of the stereotypical female role.

The *social-inequity theory* of female depression is espoused by those who emphasize the discrimination against women in work, education, and marriage (Radloff, 1975). This discrimination, they note, leads to chronic low self-esteem, low aspirations, real helplessness, dependency on others, and clinical depression. These real social inequities make it difficult for women to achieve mastery by direct action and assertion. The implied "treatment" for social inequities on a societal level is political, legal, and social change; on a personal level it is the development of technical skills.

The *learned-helplessness model* emphasizes that the stereotypical ideas of femininity create in women a cognitive and emotional set against assertion and independence. This helplessness, which is learned early and is reinforced by society, is the prototype of depression (Seligman, 1975). Embodied in this view is the belief that women are trained not to be aggressive but are then devalued for being passive and dependent. The treatment for learned helplessness is the development of emotional awareness of the condition, that is, "raising one's consciousness," as well as direct cognitive change— learning to be independent and not helpless.

SELF-HELP GROUPS

One proposed treatment for helplessness is self-help, and self-help groups have become popular among women. The idea of small groups of persons with common problems working together to achieve a specific goal antedates the women's movement (Marsh, 1931; Dumont, 1974). Alcoholics Anonymous is one of the best-known of the self-help groups, which have expanded to the overweight, the lonely, nursing mothers, problem drinkers, gamblers, homosexuals, runaway youths, widows, single parents, the divorced, mental patients, unemployed women, child abusers. In the last five years there has been a remarkable growth in these peer-oriented groups. While the diverse composition of these groups defies any serious generalization, Dumont (1974), in attempting to organize self-help groups in Massachusetts, has identifed underlying themes that are useful to review.

He notes that self-help groups are rooted in the American tradition. Group affiliation creates a source of cohesion and a sense of optimism that change is possible through community affiliation and grass-roots hard work. The groups have been given impetus by the community mental health movement. This movement pointed out the role of social disorganization in the development of mental illness and challenged the label of "disease," arguing that mental disorders are forms of social deviance and problems in living that can best be treated by the patient's neighbors rather than by professionals who distance themselves by their education. Peer influence is used to maximize change in the undesired behavior through identification and role modeling and by offering the reward of a meaningful socialization experience.

Although a scholarly literature exists on theoretical aspects of small groups (Astrachan, 1970; Singer et al., 1975), there has been little study of the self-help movement by professionals. Little information is available on the nature of the different groups, their effects, and whom they serve.

Against this background I would like to describe two different types of self-help groups—one task-oriented toward improving skills and teaching women to be less helpless (Women's Educational and Counseling Center) and the other psychologically oriented toward making women conscious of the forces in society which presumably keep them helpless (consciousness-raising). I have been directly involved with the first group as part of a research study. The information on consciousness-raising is secondhand, from reading and testimonials of friends who have at times displayed impressive behavioral changes.

Becoming Less Helpless as Therapy (Women's Educational and Counseling Center)

The Women's Educational and Counseling Center is a self-help center for women with a college education. It offers career-related services including information about employment, education, career development, child care, and sponsors groups for women with such related concerns as reentry into a career after child-rearing. It is staffed by volunteers, some of whom have professional training and many of whom have come through the program.

The users include educated married women who typically have had an interrupted career or education because of moves resulting from their husbands' professional advancements or from child-rearing. Other women come because of a conscious rethinking of roles, either a wish to overcome boredom and social isolation they felt in housework, or after direct involvement in a women's group.

We undertook to survey the applicants at the center when the director of the group expressed concern about the number of applicants who seemed depressed. We surveyed 100 consecutive applicants and assessed their clinical status using the same systematic techniques we had applied to patients coming for treatment to the Yale Depression Research Unit outpatient clinic. We also followed the applicants over a four-month period.

About a third of the applicants had mild to moderate symptoms and about 20 percent would probably have been accepted for outpatient treatment with antidepressants (Weissman et al., 1973). However, when we compared the individual symptoms of the counseling center's depressed applicants, whom we termed the normal depressives, with a matched group of women under treatment with antidepressants at the Yale Depression Research Unit, we discovered certain important differences (Weissman, Prusoff, and Pincus, 1975). The normal depressives were similar to the depressed patients in disturbances of mood, but not in symptom pattern. The normal depressives had a relative absence of somatic complaints and somatic anxiety. Moreover, during the next four months none of the normal depressives received psychiatric treatment or medication; all of them worked out a career or educational plan for themselves and all of them were asymptomatic. The normal depressives attributed their symptoms to feeling lonely, dislocated, having recently moved, being in a state of transition. They attributed their improvement to practical help and group support through a transitional period.

Without an appropriate experimental design we can only speculate. It may be that the direct assistance offered by the center helped
to hasten the women's adaptation, prevented the development of
symptoms into a full-blown depressive syndrome, and avoided the
necessity of psychiatric treatment.

Several points emerged that warrant further study. Women's self-
help groups like this one probably include a number of women with
preclinical or early depressive disorders. If the group can help the
women overcome helplessness and find a way to achieve new skills
and develop a sense of mastery, then the group experience can have
important implications for prevention.

Raising Consciousness as Therapy

Another alternative to traditional therapy for women is the consciousness-raising (C.R.) group. These groups began to sprout during
the early 1970s. Unlike the self-help group that emphasized skills,
C.R. groups are concerned with the social roots of women's helplessness. According to Martha Kirkpatrick (1975), C.R. groups are an
outgrowth of a social technique used during the revolution in China.
Women's organizations were formed to encourage women to resist
traditional bondage to husband and family and to become competent
and independent.

The traditional C.R. group is small, six to ten members, leaderless,
and has the goal of examining each member's social condition and its
ramification in her personal life. Members encourage one another
to become aware, to challenge, and to intervene in those conditions
that limit their personal freedom and action. The C.R. groups were
adopted by persons involved in the women's movement because of
dissatisfaction with traditional therapies, which were seen as male-
dominated, anti-women, and which encouraged women to accept a
submissive role.

C.R. groups have some similarities to traditional therapies (Table
4). There is opening up, sharing of feelings and opinions in a supportive and confidential relationship. Improvement of morale and
an increase in self-esteem are the overall goals.

There are, however, important differences. The C.R. group is

TABLE 4

Comparison of Traditional Psychotherapies and Consciousness-Raising Groups

Traditional Psychotherapies	Consciousness-Raising Group
Improve morale and self-esteem.	Improve morale and self-esteem.
Confidential relationship with therapist.	Confidential relationship with group members.
Supportive relationship.	Supportive relationships.
Power in therapist.	Power in group.
Therapist is in charge.	Leaderless.
Problems are related to inner dynamics.	Problems are related to society.
Emphasis on personal problems.	Emphasis on society, economics and politics.
Therapist defines goals.	Group members define goals.
Change the person to adjust to society.	Change members' perceptions and change society.
Talking.	Social action, talking, and listening.
Source of discomfort is internal.	Source of discomfort is in society.
Patient-therapist unequal.	Peer equality.

leaderless, emphasizes peer equality, and relates the women's problems to social, economic, and political problems of the women's minority status. Most important, the C.R. group starts with the assumption that environmental, rather than intrapsychic, dynamics play the major role in the person's difficulties (Kirsh, 1974). Moreover, the consumers of C.R. groups are not usually seeking therapy. Women who attend have reported more independence, confidence, higher ambition, and general well-being. Consciousness-raising groups could be alternative mental health resources for preventing depression in women. They present intriguing possibilities for preventing that portion of depression that may be associated with women's role. Unfortunately, the efficacy of C.R. groups is largely unstudied (Waskow, 1974).

CONCLUSION

There is no doubt that women have more depression, both treated and untreated. There is good evidence that traditional treatments, both pharmacotherapy and psychotherapy, have value. Drugs essentially reduce the acute symptoms of depression and prevent their return; psychotherapy enhances interpersonal satisfaction and adjustment in the major roles. These treatments, however, do not touch the basic cause of depression and have achieved little in terms of primary prevention. If anything, the rates of mild depression in women, as seen in outpatient clinic attendance and suicidal attempts, have increased. At least one reason for the predominance of depressed women may be related to social inequality and learned helplessness. The remedy for learned helplessness, in fact, may be self-help. Self-help can come in several forms: improving skills, acting less helpless, expecting less helplessness, and changing institutions and beliefs that encourage helplessness. The very act of self-help invariably reduces helplessness.

Experience with at least one of these groups showed that many of the users were mildly depressed when they came for help and were asymptomatic after they had worked out a plan that left them feeling less helpless. This is, of course, not experimental evidence. Testimonial or even pre- and post-therapy ratings of self-selected samples cannot be considered evidence by careful investigators. On the other hand, the concept of self-help for learned helplessness has a certain intuitive appeal. The predominance of depressed women is a numerical fact. C.R. groups, as the sole therapy, probably would not be too helpful and certainly not as rapid as antidepressants for the full-blown syndrome of depression. Self-help groups require more energy, engagement, and optimism than someone with a moderate clinical depression can muster, but the groups may help prevent more serious symptoms in many dissatisfied, unhappy, and lonely women. They may also be useful as an adjunct to therapy following symptom reduction. Self-help groups are certainly as difficult to evaluate as the traditional psychotherapies, probably even more so since women in the movement share a distrust of behavioral scientists (Kravetz, 1974). However, a deeper understanding of nontraditional therapies like women's self-help groups and a critical evaluation of their role in preventing mental disorders and in delivering mental health services are both timely and warranted.

REFERENCES

Astrachan, B. M. 1970. Towards a social systems model of therapeutic groups. *Social Psychiatry*, 5:110-119.

Auerbach, A., Luborsky, L., and Johnson, M. 1972. Clinicians' predictions of outcome of psychotherapy: A trial of a prognostic index. *Am. J. Psychiatry*, 128:830-835.